POLICY AND PRACTICE IN EDUCATION

NUMBER SIXTEEN

INDUCTION:

FOSTERING CAREER DEVELOPMENT AT ALL STAGES

POLICY AND PRACTICE IN EDUCATION

1: Lindsay Paterson, *Education and the Scottish Parliament* (out of print)
2: Gordon Kirk, *Enhancing Quality in Teacher Education* (out of print)
3: Nigel Grant, *Multicultural Education in Scotland* (out of print)
4: Lyn Tett, *Community Education, Lifelong Learning and Social Inclusion* (Second edition, 2006)
5: Sheila Riddell, *Special Educational Needs* (Second edition, 2006)
6: J. Eric Wilkinson, *Early Childhood Education: The New Agenda* (2003)
7: Henry Maitles, *Values in Education: We're All Citizens Now* (2005)
8: Willis Pickard and John Dobie, *The Political Context of Education after Devolution* (2003)
9: Jim O'Brien, Daniel Murphy and Janet Draper, *School Leadership* (2003)
10: Margaret Nicolson and Matthew MacIver (eds), *Gaelic Medium Education* (2003)
11: Gordon Kirk, Walter Beveridge and Iain Smith, *The Chartered Teacher* (2003)
12: Jim O'Brien, *The Social Agenda of the School* (not yet published, 2007)
13: Ann Glaister and Bob Glaister (eds), *Inter-agency Collaboration: Providing for Children* (2005)
14: Mary Simpson, *Assessment* (2005)
15: Ian Menter, Estelle Brisard and Ian Smith, *Convergence or Divergence? Initial Teacher Education in Scotland and England* (2006)
16: Janet Draper and Jim O'Brien, *Induction: Fostering Career Development at All Stages* (2006)
17: Sheila Riddell and Lyn Tett, *Gender and Teaching: Where Have All the Men Gone?* (2006)

POLICY AND PRACTICE IN EDUCATION

SERIES EDITORS
JIM O'BRIEN and CHRISTINE FORDE

INDUCTION:
FOSTERING CAREER DEVELOPMENT AT ALL STAGES

Janet Draper
School of Education and Lifelong Learning,
University of Exeter

and

Jim O'Brien
Vice Dean, Moray House School of Education,
University of Edinburgh

DUNEDIN ACADEMIC PRESS
EDINBURGH

Published by
Dunedin Academic Press Ltd
Hudson House
8 Albany Street
Edinburgh EH1 3QB
Scotland

ISBN 1 903765 55 2
ISBN 13: 978-1-903765-55-5
ISSN 1479-6910

British Library Cataloguing in Publication data
A catalogue record for this book is available from the British Library

Typeset by Makar Publishing Production
Printed in Great Britain by Cromwell Press

CONTENTS

SERIES EDITORS' INTRODUCTION

The establishment of a national induction scheme for new entrants to the teaching profession in Scotland is one of the most significant developments in teacher policy in recent years. It has rapidly become part of the landscape in education. Drawing from their own research, conducted over a number of years, Janet Draper and Jim O'Brien provide us with a critical account of the development of practice in this area.

The authors indicate a number of key issues concerning the purpose, design and management of induction programmes to be considered by policy makers and by those in local authorities and schools directly involved in managing and supporting induction programmes.

The use of international examples and research findings allow us to appreciate the multifaceted nature of induction. The authors move beyond the present Scottish focus on induction for newly qualified teachers and explore the process of induction in relation to the different transition points in teachers' careers, for example as they move schools or posts. As work patterns become more diverse such transitions will feature more frequently, requiring induction to be a planned and resourced programme in schools. At a time when schools seek to maximise effective teaching, this book helps us address the central question of how best to support teachers to continue to make their best contribution to pupil learning whilst they are dealing with significant change themselves.

Dr Jim O'Brien
Vice Dean and Director,
Centre for Educational Leadership,
Moray House School of Education,
The University of Edinburgh

Dr Christine Forde
Senior Lecturer in Educational Studies
The University of Glasgow

ACKNOWLEDGEMENTS

This book would not have been possible if it had not been for the work, energy and enthusiasms of a range of colleagues who have worked with us over the years. We recognise and thank all those teachers who have participated willingly in surveys and case study work. We owe a great deal to the General Teaching Council for Scotland which supported the studies. We have benefited greatly from discussion, challenge and debate with a range of colleagues especially in the Moray House School of Education in the University of Edinburgh and such interactions have resulted in this book. In particular our thinking and views on induction have been greatly informed and influenced by several people: namely Fiona Christie, Helen Fraser, Paquita McMichael, Stephen Sharp and Warwick Taylor.

Chapter1

WHAT IS INDUCTION FOR?

Preamble

In this book we explore the experience of induction: what it is for, how it is done and why. The concept of induction has recently been hijacked in education and has been used exclusively to refer to beginning teachers, but induction as a process has been widely studied beyond teaching and well beyond early beginnings in work. There has also been a tendency to see it as a bounded experience in teaching, framed by a set period of time and the provision of resources for support and a set standard to be achieved. In this book induction will be considered as playing a role in enabling career transitions, characterised by all the variation and uncertainties that accompany individual change. From the wider study of induction it is clear that effective induction is a multi-stage process that makes significant demands on all staff who are involved. It may be understood as an entitlement and as good human resource management practice and as a force for development and for retention.

At a time when there is concern about retention in teaching and when the demographics of the profession inevitably mean many new staff will be entering teaching, induction policy and practice become high stakes in ensuring as adequate supply of teachers who are committed and supported in their professional development. The Organisation for Economic Co-operation and Development study (OECD, 2002, p. 169) notes 'Teacher policy needs to ensure that teachers work in an environment which facilitates success.' Studies of induction reveal that there are real differences in teacher experiences and especially in teacher experiences in the early time in a new post. For many, there is a greater likelihood of early difficulties rather than early success being experienced, and this is an unwelcome situation especially given the established link between early success and teacher retention (Johnson and Birkeland, 2003).

In its developed form, transition at work is seen as having several dimensions that have direct implications for induction systems. New staff need to be socially integrated into the work group or professional community. They need help to 'learn the ropes', they have professional development needs that need to be met and the process of changing post may impact on their professional identity. For all of these they may need support. In schools we now pay considerable attention to the process of transition of pupils/students between schools, acknowledging that it takes young people time to settle in to a new school and learn the ropes. This book argues that we should do the same for staff.

Taking up a new post

Taking up a new post is a time of uncertainty, when new demands and new expectations must be confronted and handled. Even confident individuals may have moments of being unsure whether they will cope and even those who are well prepared for a new post will find they face unexpected pressures. For those who are less confident the effects are likely to be greater. Self theory and research suggests that however confident we may be in a familiar situation, a new situation has the potential to take us out of our 'comfort zone'. Self esteem which derives from our relative success in previous situations is put at risk by the move to a new post and there is no guarantee that any success will transfer. Self esteem helps us to cope with change but threats to our self esteem expose us and make us more vulnerable (Burns, 1982). Self esteem is threatened by a move to a new post (Hopson, 1986) . . . just when we need that self esteem to support us in coping with the new situation.

Is all this inevitable?

It has been argued (Schein, 1988; Nicholson and West, 1988) that a good induction experience can be helpful in reducing the impact of the change to a new situation. Information and preparation can smooth the path, support coping and establish a base for professional learning in the new situation. By having as clear a view as possible of the new situation we can recognise demands, draw on relevant transferable skills and understandings and prepare to develop new capacities. A realistic preview of the post is important. Misunderstandings and misconceptions are unhelpful and, by needing to be overcome for effective working, waste valuable time and energy that could be spent settling in and achieving early success in post. Early effectiveness and success (Schein, 1988) in its turn supports positive and competent views of the self which makes adjusting to change easier.

The purpose of induction is thus to smooth the passage into a new post, not only because humanely this makes for a good early experience for the new incumbent but because it make sense in economic as well as human terms. New staff are more likely to work effectively and to do so sooner, they are more likely to be retained (and thus save further recruitment, selection and induction costs), there is an opportunity to clearly define the nature of the work to be done, to capitalise on the strengths and to identify and address the development needs of the new incumbent.

Induction into work is recognised as having multiple significance. In human terms induction helps people settle in to a new work setting, to become clear about what is expected of them, what and where they can contribute and what support and development opportunities are available. In managerial terms, induction is important in aiding efficient and effective use of staff time. If people know what they are to do, how they will be supported and what the key priorities, policies and procedures are in the work context they are then more likely to work effectively. In organisational terms effective induction can help new staff integrate and helps to acculturate new staff into the work context. Good induction is thus enabling. Poor induction on the other hand leaves new starters at whatever stage with insufficient information and understanding to resolve how to work effectively. It is unsurprising therefore that there is clear evidence that induction affects commitment and retention (Johnson and Birkeland, 2003). Effective induction which enables new staff to work effectively and make fewer mistakes (through ignorance) is more likely to support the development of positive attitudes to the employing organisation, and to the learning opportunities inherent in a new post leading to commitment and a greater likelihood of staff being retained. Poor induction leaves staff feeling unsupported and confused and unsure of what aspects of the job are most important. It is little wonder that they may then feel little commitment and little desire to stay.

The broader significance of induction derives from several factors, including the contribution of education to economic growth and the impact of major workforce reforms, the changing nature of teachers' work, recognition of the need for good opportunities for professional development, and of the significance of the first year of teaching for subsequent attitudes to professional development, the link between personal and professional development and the importance of collegial and collaborative development. Good induction can thus lay the basis for future professional development, and it is important that expectations for professional development reflect those developmental processes found to be most effective in enhancing professional practice. Time for professional development will always be limited for teachers whose key commitment is to the learning of others and thus it must be used well. Poor induction by contrast is more likely to lead to early experience of work within which a developmental dimension is absent.

What is induction?

Defining induction opens up a number of interesting issues. Induction is defined (Chambers, 1990) as two verbs:

To *induce*: to bring in, draw on, to bring into being, to initiate or speed up;

To *induct*: to introduce, to put in possession, to install.

Induction as a noun reflects both of these: installation in office, an introductory scene, reasoning from particular cases to general solutions.

All of these help us to understand the early period in taking up a new post! New staff are drawn in, they are initiated and, with good induction, they are perhaps speeded up. They are put in possession of essential information and contacts, they build their own understandings of their work and workplace from particular experiences and the quality and representativeness of those experiences is important.

Induction has been explored in many ways but at its core induction can enable staff to settle into new posts and become effective within them. Staff are chosen for a post on the grounds that they seem suited to its demands. But taking up a new post is not straightforward, for there is in the first instance

- a need to understand and meet expectations some of which may be specific to the context;
- a need for information about the context and the policies and procedures which operate within it, some of which may be specific to that context;
- a need to integrate into the staff team in order to both have access to collegial support and to make a contribution;
- an opportunity for development.

The desired outcomes of induction lend themselves to analysis that draws upon key theories in education. A good grasp of key expectations, policies and personnel will enable the new arrival to work positively and this requires an understanding of the context, the work expected, the criteria for success and the sources of support and feedback available. In constructivist terms the new arrival must build an understanding in order to recognise key dimensions and requirements of the work. With the support of more experienced staff the new arrival will be able operate beyond their current field of full understanding. In Brunerian terms a well-organised induction programme will provide scaffolds to support the process of building understanding and developing practice. Useful support will enable new staff to build an accurate understanding earlier than those without such support. These understandings will then guide the newly arrived teacher in making the myriad decisions which are part of the teacher's role.

An alternative approach which also yields useful insights on induction is the work of Lave and Wenger (1991). In their view learning is situated, that is, it is embedded in its context. Membership of a professional learning community allows individuals to share their understandings and to benefit from the understandings of others. It follows therefore that integration into the professional learning community is important for new arrivals in order that professional progress may be made. Findings on professional learning suggest collaborative professional development is more effective than purely individual efforts and this raises the significance of the collegial context. Although Hargreaves (1994) has suggested that there are dangers in enforced or contrived collegiality, other studies (for example, EPPI, 2004; King and Newmann, 2001) have suggested that where collaboration is real it creates a fertile context for development and one function of induction is thus to integrate the new arrival into the professional learning community.

Induction for all

Much of the exploration of induction in education has focused on new teachers, or beginning or probationer teachers and thus has highlighted induction into the whole experience of professional formation, that is, of becoming a teacher. This is clearly important because the early years are crucial, a time of 'complex behavioural and conceptual learning and thus of intensive professional development' (Kelchtermans and Ballet, 2002, p. 10) and a time when professional identity is forming and developing. Given the importance of the early period in post, induction has thus come to be regarded in teaching as something special for novices.

But induction is not only for beginning teachers. It is also important for those who change roles within and between schools, since new roles require new ways of working and new understandings of systems and offer new opportunities for innovation and learning and for drawing upon past experience. The move into management roles is but one case in point. Here the role changes, usually taking on more of a whole-school focus than before, and the reactions of colleagues change. New elements of the system must be understood and some may benefit from change. For the arrival of new staff has the potential to invigorate an organisation: supporting people simply to fit in is a recipe for stagnation.

In teaching, induction is needed at any time when staff take up a new post whether it be in the same or a new (or first) school, and whether or not it involves a promotion or a horizontal shift in role. For if role or school (or both) change there is a need to settle in, in order to work effectively and make a contribution.

Kelchtermanns (1993) argues that teachers develop a personal interpretive framework comprising two parts: a professional self and subjective educational theory, or the individual's system of knowledge about teaching (and schools). The move to a new role throws into question the existing professional self and raises questions about coping with new expectations (which may in themselves be more or less clear). New situations may also threaten confidence in subjective educational theory, since past success may not carry over to the new situation, and new incumbents of rather different posts, for example, management or specialist posts in special educational needs, may find their subjective educational theory is not easily applicable to the demands of new situations.

A further effect of moving post is its impact upon identity. Poppleton and Riseborough (1990) found that work was central to many teachers' lives. Similar findings come from the Meaning of Work studies (1987) which compared the work centrality of ten occupational groups. Teachers ranked third highest on their measures of work centrality. Ball makes the link between teaching work and identity when he explores the impact of performativity on 'teachers' souls' (2003). The longitudinal study conducted by Day and others of teachers' identities and lives suggested that teachers' professional and personal identities were influenced by changes in the policy and professional development contexts (Day, 2004). Studies of early professional formation have reflected a recognition of the role teaching plays in teachers' views of self. McNally's recent work (2006) explores the ways in which new teachers identities develop, citing emotionality and relationality as key elements of the process. On emotionality he found feelings and fears ran high as new teachers struggled to come to terms with the reality of teaching every day. The social context of school, and the relationships developed with colleagues and pupils are also key to the process, he argues. He also suggested that much learning in the early stages of working is through informal means, which is why social integration into the professional community or community of practice is so important, and why those who began teaching on temporary contracts and moved from school to school were so disadvantaged (Draper *et al.*, 1998a).

Over time and through career, identity is further shaped by career decisions and associated actions: some aspire to climb a vertical career ladder, while others reject this and particularly reject an identity of themselves as managers (Draper and McMichael, 1998a; 2000b). But the link is complex. While identity is shaped by role and experience, it also shapes aspirations. One study (Draper and McMichael, 2000b) of those who were subject department heads and others who were assistant headteachers explored different facets of the teachers' identities (subject, career, management, out of school, disenchantment) and found that it was not role but career intention which distinguished identities. Those who were assistant heads and those who aspired to be so were more similar in identity than those who held the same post (be it subject head or assistant head). In a sense the aspiring subject heads were 'assistant heads in waiting' in terms of their identities.

Taking up a new post is therefore a potentially vulnerable time for identity, when it may be shaped or tested. Part of the role of induction is thus to support successful integration into a new role, sustaining identity (partly through success) and opening the way for further development.

What does 'settling in' involve?

Settling into work in a school environment has much in common with settling in to other kinds of work. New staff need to know

- who the people are;
- how the system(s) actually works;

- what is expected;
- what the (important) rules are;
- what and who are to be found where (geographical familiarisation);
- who is the best source of what kind of help/information;

as well as

- how to do the job well, which in turn requires knowing what criteria will be used to evaluate success.

In Kelchtermann's terms settling in is likely to require some adjustments to the professional self and possibly also to subjective educational theory. The extent to which this process is under the control of the teacher may thus be relevant, as is the extent to which the new teacher can shape what they do and can contribute to the school.

Research on induction (Lacey, 1977; Draper *et al.*, 1997b; Tickle, 2000a; 2000b) has suggested that a *broad* understanding of induction is required which encompasses all these elements of induction:

- socialisation;
- organisational familiarisation and sensitisation, including key policies and priorities;
- appropriately and individually focused developmental support;
- the identification of scope for contribution.

The need for careful consideration of induction was highlighted by Lacey's early work (1977) on teacher socialisation. Lacey questioned the assumption that probation/induction should be regarded as a time when the adequacy of teacher training could be assessed by the extent to which new teachers coped. Instead he saw the early period in teaching as a significant experience in its own right and one where the context and culture of teachers' work was highly influential. Lacey also reported Wiseman and Start's (1965) findings of discontinuity in measures of teaching at the end of training, successful performance in first post, in promotion and in subsequent satisfaction with teaching. While there have been calls to seek to ensure 'continuity' between initial teacher education (ITE) and first post, the work of Draper *et al.* in Scotland (1988–91) suggested that a disjunction inevitably arose between ITE and first post for several reasons, including the need to understand the individual school as a working organisation and differences between the student teacher's and the teacher's role.

Draper *et al.* (1991) found that a real or actual school was experienced by new teachers to be very different from a generalised notional school, or indeed from specific schools experienced during the period of ITE. Each school it had its own peculiarities and ways of doing things to which a new teacher had to become sensitised. Ball (1994) identified similar phenomena as the 'micropolitics' of the school and Kuzmic (1994) wrote of the need to develop 'organisational literacy'. The fact that for some this was their first experience of working could add to the difficulty of the task.

Louis (1980) made an early and a useful distinction by separating out different aspects of taking up a new post. He distinguished 'change', the difference between past and new experience of work from 'surprise', the difference between what is expected of a post and the reality which is actually experienced. Effective induction will clarify the nature of a post, reduce surprise and enable the new incumbent to adjust and develop.

In relation to differences in role, beginning teachers carry major responsibility for their pupils' learning to a far higher degree than during ITE and Draper *et al.* (1991) found that the reality of this overwhelmed some and for most it altered their sense of the work they were doing. Veenman (1984) first drew attention to the 'reality shock' awaiting new teachers as they took full control of classes for the first time. Huberman (1993), when studying the transition from teacher education to teaching, called this 'praxis shock', a term used later by Kelchtermanns and Ballet (2002). The effects of this shock have also been held to impact on subsequent career development. (Sikes *et al.*, 1985).

The recent sharp focus on classrooms and classroom practice to the virtual exclusion of the wider role and contexts of teachers' work, for example, working with colleagues and parents in the wider 'educationist context' (Keddie, 1971), has possibly obscured the breadth of the role which new teachers must master and the need to become familiar with and to master all aspects of the teacher's role within its specific context, for the role embraces more than teaching and learning concerns. As Forde *et al.* (2006, p. 161) note, 'In the 21st century a teacher is an active professional, liaising and collaborating with a number of other professionals managing not only learning and teaching in their own classrooms but also managing other staff such as para professionals.'

These examples of discontinuity reinforce Lacey's position that early teaching cannot be regarded as simply a test-bed for the evaluation of ITE, since the specific context also shaped the new teacher's capacity to cope. To further complicate matters, Draper *et al.* (1991) also found that while many reported that they had been well trained in a number of areas this did not mean they found them easy to handle in practice and, in contrast, there were areas for which they felt training had given them little preparation and which yet proved non-problematical. The induction period was flavoured by the specific context which generated its own issues. Bullough (1997) concurs but also argues that the teacher is not simply passive and receptive, but brings his or her own experience and beliefs to the process of making sense of the new situation. Lacey highlighted that teachers found different strategies for coping within their early time in post: specifically he suggests some genuinely reshape themselves to fit their work context (internalisation), others strategically (appear to) comply while others seek to change and redefine their situation. There may be different ways of coping therefore as well as different amounts of pressure to conform to the current context, which suggests that induction may need to be individualised.

The very need for induction reflects the amount of learning and adjustment that is required of the new teacher in post, and the argument pursued in this book is that this need for induction arises whenever there is a significant change in post at any career stage whether or not it involves a change of school.

Many teachers in the Probation study (Draper *et al.*, 1991) also reported that their overwhelming experience during their early time in post could not be easily described as developmental but was shaped rather more by a sense of having to prove they were competent. They felt they had to cope and to be seen to cope. Summative assessment contributed to this and because they were often not sure of how well they were doing they were unclear about how best to proceed. But to ask for help was to imply deficiency even though the rhetoric of probation was developmental. The micropolitics of induction are thus part of the story.

Tickle (2000a; 2000b) identifies the role of induction as introducing new teachers to their work settings and supporting them in their adjustment. He offers the metaphor, albeit one that he believes is limiting, of a bridge between professional learning during initial preparation (Initial teacher education, ITE, or training, ITT) and the professional learning which takes place once in post. This reflects the continuity that was sought for many years between ITE and first post. But he also identifies that new teachers bring strengths and potential contribution to schools, so part of induction is enabling new teachers to make a unique contribution, rather than simply being seen as deficient. Kuzmic (1994) developed the idea of 'organisational literacy' as a dimension of induction, suggesting that alongside socialisation there is need to develop empowerment, the capacity to impact on the school. It is not enough to be able to teach well, he says, it is also important to understand the setting in which one works, to be able to make effective use of what is offered and to build on it.

The contribution which new staff can make is also important. Past experience in or out of teaching may be useful to the school if opportunities are made available to give to as well as take from induction. New entrants to teaching bring many different characteristics. Gatherer (2003) noted that teachers are a vibrant group, some entering early in their careers while others come into the profession with considerable work experience from elsewhere. Induction cannot therefore be a unitary experience since, for some, the early time in teaching is about learning about working full time for the first time as well as learning about teaching, while for others it may be a mix of learning about working in schools *as a teacher* (and how that differs from previous work experience) and learning about teaching. Where they are the same is that all also have their own experiences understandings and enthusiasms to offer and an effective induction process should explore and enable these.

Induction is not only important as a means of enhancing commitment and retention. It also offers an opportunity to reinforce desirable ways of working. In teaching in particular there is an expectation that teachers will engage in professional development. It is important therefore that early experience in post reflects that expectation. There will of course be a sharp learning curve in any new post. However professional learning needs and professional development opportunities both need to be explored in the early time in post to reinforce and model this expectation otherwise it runs the risk of appearing to be rhetoric devoid of reality.

A model of induction

Nicholson and West (1988) reviewed induction experiences and offered a useful four-stage model of the process of settling in. They argue that the first stage is 'preparation' which occurs in the period prior to taking up a post. During this stage information (for example, on policies and procedures) is given to clarify the nature of the work and the organisational setting. This stage, which includes the new recruit's experiences of recruitment and selection processes, helps to prepare the new member of staff for the demands that will be made and assists in the development of a realistic set of expectations about the post, which should reduce 'surprise'. Following preparation comes the 'encounter' stage during the earliest days in post where preliminary understandings are developed which may be changed by subsequent experiences. A rudimentary 'map' of the post and its context, especially its interpersonal context, is developed. The third stage of adjustment, that may take several months (or longer), refines and elaborates the initial impressions. The fourth stage, called 'stabilisation', is where the new post is seen as current rather than new work. The new incumbent is sufficiently settled into the post to begin to look ahead and seek new opportunities for development and change. Survival and adjustment belong in the past. At this stage, which has some parallel with Maslow's (1954) self-actualisation level, the individual is freer to develop and learn and there is more scope for making the contribution to which Tickle (2000a) in particular refers.

Complex professional work is particularly affected by the quality of induction, partly because of the many competing priorities in complex work and partly because the initial period of working is usually understood to be a time of intense professional development where skills and understanding previously honed during initial professional training are put to the test in a real work context. In addition, in public sector professional work the changing nature of working, with increased accountability, greater centralisation and reduced trust in professionals sharpen the uncertainties of new starters and add significantly to the expected initial fast learning curve and impact on long-term commitment to professional development. A clear example arises in the case of teaching where a 'deluge of directives' raises the level of uncertainty. The teacher is faced with a dilemma: long-term professional development is perceived as part of the job of a professional teacher yet the world of work in which they find themselves changes so fast that it is difficult to engage in learning which may be only for the short term.

Of late, with demographic changes, the ageing profile of the teaching profession in many developed countries and some concern being voiced about future teacher supply, the retention of teachers is increasingly being recognised as important. This is against a backdrop of many more job alternatives than before for those who might traditionally have followed a teaching career and increasing recognition of the costs of recruiting, training and replacing teachers. (Darling-Hammond, 1990). In a rapidly changing world, there is an expectation that lifelong learning is an integral part of an economically competitive society. This inevitably means that professional development is necessary to ensure that teachers are up to date. Hoyle's distinction between restricted and extended professionals (1969) where the latter see professional development and improvement of practice as part of the job is increasingly inapplicable to teaching. Already in some situations professional development is perceived as an entitlement and as a source of motivation, in others it remains an obligation but increasingly it is understood as part of teachers' work. Key variations arise between systems in the extent to which time for professional development is built into the design of teachers' work or left for teachers to find opportunities in their 'own time'.

Evidence accumulated that induction for beginning teachers was limited (for example, in Scotland, Draper *et al.* (1991; 1997b) and in England, Tickle (2000a), Bubb *et al.*, 2002)), that beginning teachers were less supported than was helpful or intended and that their development needs and their significance in the education system were not highly rated. One consequence of this was that new teachers struggled to cope, being left to sink or swim. A few received excellent support but many had little.

What should induction provide?

Evidence on induction in general suggests that good induction offers opportunities for early success in post to sustain confidence and positive attitudes to the work. This has direct implications for the management of teaching, for example, the class(es) allocated to a new teacher (preferably not the classes no one else wants to teach) and the extent to which a newcomer can take up a role which is free of uncompleted tasks which have awaited their arrival. There should be opportunities for a newcomer to be well prepared to take up the post. This requires advance information, a realistic preview of the post, prior training and development where needed and significant and appropriate support for learning once in post.

Induction may be understood in many different ways:

- as a period of time where new staff are allowed not to know about the organisation;
- as a set of supportive experiences;
- as a route for early feedback and review;
- as a requirement;
- as an entitlement;
- as an obligation on employers;
- as an opportunity for learning;
- as a trial by fire (proving competence);
- as an investment in new staff;
- as an extended process of staff selection;
- as a time when identity may be further shaped;
- as a time when support is offered for development.

Many of these are self-explanatory. Two key aspects will be explored in more depth and in combination:

- induction as a time of proving competence or of developing practice which links to fitting a prescribed pattern of practice and developing as an individual teacher;
- induction as a time where support is offered.

Induction as time of proving competence or developing practice

There will be expectations held of any new arrival in a job. These may be very specific or more open-ended. The extent to which a new arrival can meet these expectations will depend in part on how clear they are on what is expected as well as on what they are capable of doing and learning. As we saw above, in a complex job like teaching and working in school contexts that vary significantly, clarifying expectations about what is wanted was not found to be easy. New arrivals have to prove their competence, and to do so in context-specific situations. There may or may not be scope to meet the needs of the post in different ways and there may or may not be opportunities or space given to learn what is required and to develop in order to meet expectations.

A focus on proof seems more likely, or at least more overt where the beginning teacher works in a context that requires evidence of competence after the initial qualification stage. Where there is further certification, staff will be expected to show they can cope with their new post in the face of the 'reality shock' (Veenman, 1984) of starting work as a teacher. They must prove that they are competent teachers. This will be particularly the case where the context has a high level of accountability. In an era of commitment to continuing professional development (CPD), it is of course expected that induction focuses on development, that new teachers will also be given opportunities to develop their practice further.

It is reasonable to expect therefore that induction can be thought of as some balance between proof and development. While assessment of competence might be held to contribute to support for development, in practice it can also be the case that involvement in assessment may inhibit seeking support with difficulties, lest competence is seen to be in doubt (Draper *et al.*, 1991; Bubb and Earley, 2006)

In consequence, in some circumstances the two may be seen as in conflict with each other. A stronger focus on assessment may mean a weaker focus on development and on what new ideas and practice the new member of staff can contribute and vice versa. The nature of the induction experience would thus be expected to vary with the balance of proving and developing. A focus on proof will also be shaped by the assessor's expectations and the criteria used for assessment. While some criteria may facilitate the new teacher's individual development and professional autonomy to develop their practice in their own way, a heavy focus on accountability and on measurable evidence is likely to narrow the experience, as we shall see in Chapter 3. This raises the issue of the extent to which induction enables or supports the new member of staff in making a contribution by stimulating change. A study of routes into primary teaching in Scotland, prior to the new induction scheme, found that headteachers welcomed beginning teachers because, although they needed support, they brought fresh ideas and a familiarity with new ways and new resources (Draper *et al.*, 1997a). These benefits will only be realised, however, if the context enables such contribution to be made. Induction which is shaped by proof, by high direction and low autonomy, will expect the new arrival to fit in to what is required by others, and to change in whatever way is necessary to meet the system as is, to 'internalise' in Lacey's (1977) terms or at the very least to 'strategically comply'. Open opportunities to develop, giving more autonomy and less direction, will generate a sense of agency and will allow the newcomer to help shape the system and make a contribution as well as to develop in their own way as a teacher.

These issues have been explored above in relation to beginning teachers, but apply to any member of staff taking up a new post. There is a need to establish credibility and competence, but if induction only addresses what is required to 'fit in' then much will be lost.

Induction as a time where support is offered

A further variation arises in the amount of support offered. It is generally assumed that more support means more development, but the focus of that support is also important, as noted above. However it is clear also that support *per se* is not inevitably helpful. Given the variations which exist in individual teacher needs, it may be difficult to establish the most appropriate support and to match support to that need and some teachers report frustration with support being offered that is not currently relevant to their needs (Draper *et al.*, 1991; Bubb and Earley, 2006).

While each of these issues has its own contribution to make to an understanding of the induction experience, combining them opens up new ways of thinking about the induction process. Different combinations of focus on proof and of amount of support produce a series of distinct possibilities for induction and these are shown below in the model in Figure 1. High support is assumed here to be associated with outcomes of high development, but the degree of choice over the direction of development varies. Hence there may be substantial support to develop in a particular way or substantial support to develop autonomously. Alternatively there may be little support and this may be combined with specific (but hidden) expectations, hidden because with little support goals are not clarified. Or there may be no specific expectations but simply an unstructured situation. The model does not explore the extent to which practice in induction matches the rhetoric in induction, which will be considered in Chapter 3. The concern here is with induction not as a system in itself but as a process experienced by the teacher, as an aid when beginning a new post. The diagram in Figure 1 implies the two dimensions are independent and it may be that this is not the case, but for the purposes of illustration they are presented as orthogonal.

Figure 1: Combinations of support and proof/development focus

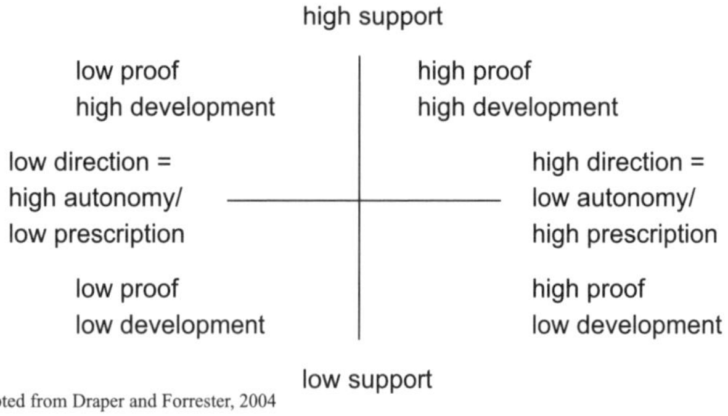

Adapted from Draper and Forrester, 2004

The initial observation is that different combinations are possible and may lead to quite different outcomes in terms of experience of induction. If it is the case that it is not just the amount of support that is important for the outcome but also the focus of that support and the extent to which a specific desirable outcome has been defined, then a more complex picture emerges. By exploring the issue of focus of support a little further a more differentiated set of outcomes can be considered, and these are illustrated in Figure 2.

Figure 2: Types of induction experience

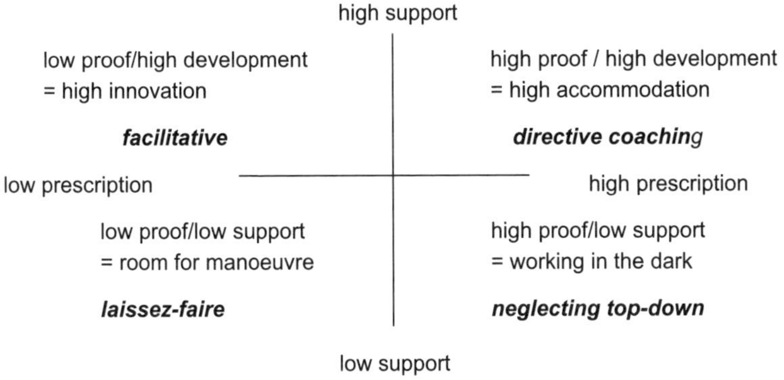

The second model unpacks variations in focus of support by the amount of autonomy the teacher has: the scope for choosing their own path of development, in combination with the level of support they receive. This might be understood as freedom to pursue an individual style or mode of performing the teacher's role. Different styles or types of induction experience are therefore identified. Such variations can be conceived of as influenced purely by individual preference or might reflect variations within departments in a school, variations in school contexts and communities, any variation indeed which questions the validity of generic prescriptions of what is to be done and how it is to be done.

Incorporating autonomy into the model in Figure 2 shifts the focus of the quadrants, away from quantity of progress made to type of progress made, and this distinguishes different sets of expectations for teachers taking up a new role. Those who are well supported may indeed all develop but the focus of that development may be more or less prescribed. At the extremes this produces quite different experiences, one flavoured by accommodation to the present norm described here as 'directive coaching' and one which supports innovation, described as 'facilitative'. For those receiving little support there is also a difference in experience: between those who have considerable room for manoeuvre which they are free to exercise, termed *laissez-faire* and those who are trying without guidance to achieve a prescribed but hidden goal, who are subject to a neglecting top-down form of experience. Similarities may be noted between these contrasting experiences and Hersey and Blanchard's model of leadership (1988) and Maccoby and Martin's (1983) model of parenting.

It is suggested here therefore that the amount of support given is not the only important dimension of induction experience: the form and focus of that support is also significant. The nature of the developmental context and the type of opportunities for development given are thus offered as important dimensions of induction. In the next chapter we will review these by considering recent changes in teachers' work and in the conceptualisation and the realisation of professional development. We shall return again to the model itself in Chapter 3 but meanwhile move in the next chapter to a consideration of induction into work and associated issues of professional development.

Chapter 2

TEACHERS' WORK AND PROFESSIONAL DEVELOPMENT

In Chapter 1 the context and the opportunities made available for professional development were highlighted. This section sets induction into work in the wider context. It will consider changes in the nature of work, especially professional and public sector work, and changing understandings of professional development. Implications for induction are identified.

Changes in work and teachers' work

Wider changes in teachers' work reflect a global agenda of restructuring and 'modernising' work that has increased accountability and central control in professional public sector work bringing significant increases in bureaucracy. Limited power has been devolved to schools.

The introduction of new induction schemes for beginning teachers can be argued to illustrate these changes very well. Although part of a global shift, individual schemes have varied, reflecting Jones and Alexiadou's (2001) suggestion that global 'travelling policies' are mediated by 'embedded practices'. Changes in teachers' work, and more specifically in arrangements for new teachers in Scotland may be seen to reflect not only wider shifts in work and careers but also the checks and balances within the Scottish system which have fashioned the ways modernisation has transpired. Major changes in Scottish teachers' work came about as a result of the McCrone Inquiry (Scottish Executive Education Department (SEED), 2000) and the subsequent associated Agreement (SEED, 2001). The outcomes of the Inquiry reflect the changes associated with modernisation interacting with concerns over teacher supply, combining a desire to modernise the profession and focus teachers on professional development while at the same time having due regard to the need to maintain a stable workforce, particularly in the face of supply problems in parts of nearby England.

Work and changes in work

While work is usually considered in terms of its outcomes and its impact on others, and teachers' work is a clear example of this, work itself has an important impact on those who work. It is well established that work plays a significant role in social identity and work remains 'significant in shaping the lives of individuals, the character of the self and social organisation' (Casey, 1995, p. 48). With changes in technology, the impact of globalisation and the development of corporate employment, expectations held about working have altered. Casey (1995) and Sennett (1998) explored changes in work and their impact on the person, and Sennett saw the end result of diminished and fragmented work opportunities as being the 'corrosion of character'. He argued that strong engagement of people with their work makes work, and the developmental and social opportunities it offers, central to their evolving identity and sense of themselves. When work changes to become less engaging and less secure, the opportunities it offers for a sense of personal progression and development are reduced. Furthermore, he suggests that an emphasis on rapid change denies the worth of what has been done and how it has been done in the past. In his conception of work he mirrors psychological analyses of motivation and the personal consequences of working and of not working. For example, the concept of higher order needs (Porter *et al.*, 1975, a redesign of Maslow's earlier hierarchy, 1954) and their satisfaction through social contact and personal development at work are reflected in his assumptions about what work has offered and should offer. So too are the latent, as opposed to the manifest financial, functions of work including sense of purpose, of mastery, of social integration and of security which were proposed by Jahoda (1982).

The concept of the 'psychological contract' is also relevant here. The term psychological contract, first coined in the 1960s, is the name given to the expectations which employers and employees have of 'their mutual obligations to each other' (Guest and Conway, 2002). It is not the same as the legal contract of employment, but rather embodies expectations of the relationship which will operate between employer and employee and how each will treat the other. Fairness, reasonableness and mutual trust are frequently used examples of such expectations. Studies (for example, Guest and Conway, 2004) have suggested that when the psychological contract is working well, commitment and satisfaction will increase and this in turn will positively influence performance. On the other hand, when one party to the relationship is held to have failed to meet obligations and expectations, for example, when professional development reviews are poorly handled or demands for tasks to be completed are perceived as unreasonable, commitment and satisfaction will be threatened and the contract will be at risk. Early understandings of psychological contracts were developed around the idea that employee commitment was exchanged for employer commitment: secure employment in a 'job for life'. Changes in patterns of employment to more temporary contracts undermine the equation of mutual commitment, one of the perceived outcomes of a positive psychological contract. The 'new deal' from employers therefore is understood to be an exchange of 'fair pay and treatment plus opportunities for training and development' (Chartered Institute of Personnel and Development (CIPD), 2006, p. 4). The CIPD concludes that 'the psychological contract provides a convincing rationale for behaving as a good employer' and emphasises that 'employment is a relationship in which the mutual obligations of employer and employee may be imprecise but have to be respected' (CIPD, 2006, p. 9). One important element in establishing this relationship is the process of induction which here must incorporate recruitment and selection processes, since they shape expectations. For it is during induction that expectations and obligations can be clarified and explored and a failure to do this may lead to unrealistically high (or low) expectations and hence to low or high levels of satisfaction and commitment.

Studies in the business world have suggested that in a knowledge economy 'human capital' is increasingly recognised as critical to success. Further research on the psychological contract (Purcell *et al.*, 2003) has suggested that effective working at a highly demanding level (high in terms of complex skills and understanding) is particularly vulnerable to the operation of the psychological contract. Where employees have considerable discretion Purcell found that they appear more likely to use that discretion effectively if they feel they are fairly treated. In consequence a recognition of psychological contracts has led to a greater concern about how staff are managed and supported in practice. It is clear from Purcell's research that good policies are not enough, they must be implemented effectively in practice to yield the desired results.

While the use of terms like 'employee' are still relatively unusual in teaching they are nonetheless an important, if often overlooked, dimension of teachers' work. Teachers are professionals and do professional work but they are also simultaneously employees, and in Scotland, most are employees of local authorities. The changes wrought by public sector modernisation may be argued to signal shifts in the psychological contract, as is evidenced in changed ways of describing working relationships, for example, in line management terms. While line managers may take day-to-day decisions which affect people at work, frequently decisions are made by those further up 'the line'. In the case of teachers this may be within or beyond the school but whatever their source these decisions impact on teachers' feelings about their work. The OECD (2002, p. 213) concluded in a comparative study of 25 countries that 'unless teachers and their representatives are actively involved in policy formulation and feel a sense of "ownership" of reform, it is unlikely that substantial changes will be implemented'. The argument for effective induction is thus strengthened further. Teachers' work is indeed high level work requiring complex skills and understanding and teachers continue to have considerable discretion about how they do their work. In Chapter 5 of this book we consider evidence which suggests that the role of induction in smoothing paths into new roles and clarifying expectations has not been adequately recognised in relation to more experienced teachers. In contrast the introduction of an elaborate induction scheme for beginning teachers could be interpreted as indicating more of a concern to assess competence than the support of new teachers as they settle into the start of a career.

Other changes have also impacted on teachers' work. One example of these is the increased participation of women in the workforce which has implications for the kinds of employment relationships being sought as well as offered, and changes in the types of contracts offered, for example, more part-time and temporary contracts rather than more open-ended contracts. For a long time teaching has had a high proportion of women workers, especially in primary schools and this has increased recently (Riddell *et al.*, 2006). Teaching posts were mainly full time but this has changed in the face of the need to manage staff costs and also because of preferences for different types of working arrangements, for example, job sharing. Part-time staffing is also used more than before, for example, to facilitate the release of teachers for management responsibilities and for in-service training/ CPD (for example, child protection, modern language teaching). Temporary contracts are also more in evidence for maternity cover, secondments, acting posts, all signs of more flexible working. A trend towards more flexible and casualised working arrangements, as highlighted in Atkinson's core/ periphery model (Atkinson, 1984; Ackroyd *et al.*, 2005), is held to result in a further loss of individual control over work, and these changes are frequently understood as an indicator of reduced commitment to staff and the attribution of reduced value to their experience in post.

Changes in professional and public sector work, shaped in part by governmental (and more global) modernisation agendas, are commonly identified as wresting central control over key elements of work through governmental and local authority micromanagement strategies, through the setting of targets and the introduction of central rather than local accountability mechanisms, all of which reduce autonomy. Ranson (2003) offers a historical analysis of the development of accountability structures in education that are reminiscent of corporate forms and argues that accountability has become a key dimension of the system rather than being simply a monitoring instrument. In such a regime, 'devolved' management may be illusory, giving an appearance of local control and freedom which are in practice undermined by central performance requirements (Ball, 2003). An associated and contributory development is the redefinition of some professional work as a set of technical tasks, requiring little in the way of complex skill or experience and incorporating little recognition of the personal and professional commitment which in the past has been taken for granted in professional work. Finally, a reduced respect for experts and a belief that some aspects of societal activity (like education) are too important to be left solely to the relevant (and possibly self-interested) professionals has resulted in reduced trust of professionals and in intervention and central direction being seen as more reasonable than hitherto (Ranson, 2003).

Much of the literature related to modernisation in teaching is drawn from the perspective of how changes occurred within the English system. While modernisation is generally seen on a global scale, the impact on England has been starkly described by many writers (Gewirtz, 2002; Ball, 2003; Ozga, 2005; Goodson and Hargreaves, 1996; Menter *et al.*, 2004). It has also been argued (Paterson *et al.*, 2001; Humes and Bryce, 2003; Raffe, 2000; Menter *et al.*, 2004) that the Scottish system is distinctive in a number of ways and one would expect that modernisation would take shape in a distinctive way in Scotland. A comparison of Scottish and English strategies for tackling supply and retention issues (Menter, 2002) suggests that the response in Scotland was more developmental, focusing on ways of supporting and rewarding teachers at work rather than structural interventions designed to extract 'more for less' from teaching staff. The Scottish response could also be considered a reflection of at least two influences: a smaller system that is easier to remodel or a more paternalistic system. On the latter point, Menter reminds readers that there are areas of concern in Scotland, not least being that of the continuing dominance and exclusiveness of the 'leadership class' so effectively outlined by Humes in 1986 and still relevant in Paterson's analysis in 1997.

Teaching as work

In considering teaching as work, Connell's (1985) rare analysis emphasised that little account had been taken of teachers themselves. Connell claimed that for a long time they were seen as mere vehicles, neutral agents of social control and social transmission, and he criticised sociologists of education for ignoring the interpersonal and individual dimension of the very human work of teaching. This might of course be seen as an inevitable consequence of classifying teachers by their group membership (gender, class, etc.) within a sociological analysis. However, in his account, a more individualised psychological approach fared no better, being criticised for focusing on the individual at the expense of noting the origins of the problems with which teachers had to deal. Connell (1985) adds support therefore to the argument pursued here that teachers' needs as employees are relatively invisible and that their views and understandings are often overlooked in the development and implementation of policy. Connell suggested little was actually known about the day-to-day experience of teachers' work and working practices, and the OECD study (2002) confirmed there were extensive research gaps on the teaching profession. Connell's analysis yielded insights on teachers' work derived from the period prior to the development of the full modernisation agenda. He saw teachers as regularly sacrificing their interests to those of 'the kids' and he argued for the importance of protecting teachers' interests, drawing upon their expertise in the processes of educational reform and recognising teachers' legitimate interest in 'the content of their jobs' and 'the control of their workplace' (Connell, 1985, p. 203).

The bulk of the literature on the impact of the modernisation agenda on teachers' work suggests these hopes went unfulfilled. In the face of limited understanding of teachers' work this is perhaps unsurprising but has the consequence that the complexity of that work has often been disregarded. The complex role of the teacher means that teaching is difficult work (Acker, 1999) which takes place in multiple settings, not exclusively in the classroom. The exposure of the educationist context (Keddie, 1971) as a significant setting of teachers' work beyond the classroom teaching context has been regularly overlooked by many, including policy makers and sometimes by teachers themselves. Some teachers have colluded with policy makers in sustaining what Nias (1989) describes as a 'bounded' view of professionalism as, for example, in MacDonald's study (2004) where she found teachers reinforced their role as classroom based and ignored or resisted engaging with their role in the educationist context of professional life outside the classroom. This tendency to 'leave the managers to manage' does not facilitate teacher participation in school or wider educational management and policy making (as promoted by OECD, 2002). In the absence of a wider understanding about teachers' work, the narrowness of a conception of teaching as almost solely classroom-based technical activity, which ignores the plurality of the teacher's role when engaging with colleagues, parents, and a range of agencies beyond the classroom makes it easier to sustain unrealistically simplistic perceptions of what is required from teachers. In the face of limited understanding of teachers' work there are significant implications for the feasibility of central control, and for the central direction of teacher activity. For induction in particular there is a clear danger of underestimating the complexity of teacher roles and hence of the demands of taking up new roles.

A further dimension of changing views of teachers' work was that current performance was not meeting and would not meet the increasing demands for highly skilled citizens in an increasingly globalised world. A significant role for professional development to change practice was thus identified. With a relatively simplistic and technicist understanding of teachers' work, a tendency to central control and a limited grasp of processes of learning, top-down models defined professional development as courses to 'update' individual teachers to meet the needs of the system. Understandings of the role of professional development and of effective forms of professional development have changed. Evidence which has accumulated on professional development suggests that more collaborative sustained teacher-centred forms of professional development are more effective in changing practice (EPPI, 2004).

Changing understandings of professional or teacher development

The position of teacher development in the conceptualisation of teaching has shifted in part in response to the impact of these wider changes and modernising efforts. This is especially the case with regard to the perceived purpose, process and location of teacher professional development within work.

Changes in the economic and social context have been offered as the basis for changes in teacher development. In its earlier forms, staff or teacher development was conceived of as a dimension of professionalism, a core element of which is considered by many (for example, Kirk, 1988) to be commitment to improvement in professional practice. This reflected a belief that initial qualification as a teacher was merely a starting-point on a career-long road of professional development. The concept of lifelong learning has also contributed to understandings of continuing professional development, moving professional development (PD) away from discrete learning experience and towards an assumption of continuing professional development (CPD) as part of teacher's work: an entitlement and an obligation.

More recently, the professional development of teachers has been championed by modernisers who believe teachers need to be updated to ensure that the economy is competitive. This view recognises education's major contribution to economic development, especially in the area of high skills development, and challenges education to constantly improve and to ensure that professional development keeps teachers abreast of changes. Bolam (1986) suggested it was useful to think about professional development needs along a continuum from system needs to individual teacher needs. Development opportunities focusing on updating on policy would be typical of a system need. Day (1999) suggested that a hierarchy existed in the ordering of professional development, with priority usually being given to system needs over school needs and school needs over individual needs. Day argued that there was a strong focus on systemic and school needs in PD opportunities to the relative exclusion of teachers' development needs. Alexandrou *et al.* (2005) offer yet another view. They argue that different types of CPD, deriving and led from different sources (system, profession and individual) are complementary at least in part, since there are common areas of interest and need. There are therefore highly contrasting views of the focus and purpose of professional development, ranging from the autonomous professional teacher committed to an individual improvement trajectory to the teacher deficient in information, understanding and, to some extent, skills whose updating is decided elsewhere.

The debate is extended by Ng (2001), who defines four main *purposes* for professional development: personal development, school development, the implementation of government policies and student learning. This flags up that individual teacher development and student learning have their place alongside more systemic development. The significance of teacher-focused development is reinforced by Duncombe and Armour's finding (2004) that development opportunities centred on teacher needs were more likely to have successful outcomes. However, they also found that while collaborative professional learning was effective, the structures and attitudes underpinning CPD did not lend themselves to such shared activity.

There is some evidence to suggest that effective collaboration may be inhibited by differences between teachers in their experience and stage of development. There is support for a stage theory of professional development (Huberman, 1993; Berliner, 2001; Wilson *et al.*, 2006), and Burbank and Kauchak (2003) draw attention to the effect of differentials in experience on the ease of collaboration.

There have also been relatively recent changes in the *process* of professional development. Professional development had been offered in two ways: as academically rooted courses which enhanced the analysis of professional values, knowledge and understanding and which led to an academic qualification at masters or doctoral level and, in contrast, courses which were intended to enhance professional practice. The recognition of informal professional development, or learning through working, as embodied in learning through self evaluation and critical reflection on teaching and on the systematic analysis of teaching, for example, through action research, opened up new vistas for professional development. The distinction between 'academic' experiences which enhanced the analysis of professional values, knowledge and understanding and courses aimed at enhancing professional practice has thus been blurred, and this is seen perhaps most clearly in the development of the Chartered Teacher programme in Scotland which combines academic and professional learning in a single learning experience. Conlon (2004) distinguished several dimensions of contrast in CPD: formal / informal; in school / out of school; externally prescribed / self-chosen which reflect the range of routes and provision of CPD and the locus of decision making about CPD. The process of identifying development needs, through formal appraisal / review or more informally and by self or other is a key dimension. This process is inevitably shaped by perceptions of the purposes noted above, and may also be shaped by the career intentions of teachers. Where needs are clearly identified the chances of relevant and useful CPD should be higher, but many questions remain about the process and tone of identifying needs as, for example, deficit or area of interest, which shape its success and teachers' receptivity to subsequent development. In a context of lifelong learning, professional development would be expected to be ongoing and the framework for CPD confirms this but nonetheless provides a limited ladder for CPD.

While a body of literature now exists on teachers' work (for example, Hargreaves, 1994; Goodson and Hargreaves, 1996; Acker, 1999), especially in England, and the role and situation of teachers is becoming better understood, teachers have nonetheless emerged as having little influence and as being expected to implement policy decided elsewhere (Day, 1999). Forde *et al.* (2006, p. 223) argue that 'most teachers who have to implement policy will not have been part of the policy or curriculum creation, or will only have had marginal involvement'. Although some teachers and their professional associations and professional bodies have played a part in policy making, the global thrust of many changes in education has meant that teachers' voices have been less heard and mechanisms for implementation in particular have often proceeded with little discussion. The recent very substantial changes in teachers' work and the central specification of how to work (for example, the literacy strategy in England) have reflected an assumption that teachers do not have their own suggestions to make and that their own professional expertise and experience is not significant, which in turn is consistent with a perception of reduced trust in experts. In Scotland, while there was consultation on the development of new Standards for Professional Development, at the implementation stage consultation faded away (Purdon, 2003b). The speedy implementation of complex arrangements for both induction and Chartered Teacher status has left little space for consultation that might have produced more streamlined and less bureaucratic arrangements. Given that the devil lies so often in the detail, the absence of consultation on that detail is telling and, one might argue, counterproductive in terms of finding ways forward that will work. This could be taken as an indication of the politicisation of teaching since it reflects a modernised and media conscious timetable with (annual accounting type) short-term goals and scanty planning as well as the controlling of activities by central bodies.

The place of teacher development in teacher's work also shows variation in that the obligatory dimension has been treated differently. Where before engagement in professional development was seen as characteristic of the 'extended professional' (Hoyle, 1969), new contractual arrangements now see it as part of the job of all teachers in some systems. In some countries it has meant that at least some time for CPD is built into working hours (for example, Scotland, Malta, Sweden) but not all. In Hong Kong, for example, while CPD is expected, time for it must be found out of working hours. However, defining CPD as part of work may only be a first step and shifts in hearts and minds and habits may take a little longer. A recent study of Scottish teachers in their fifteenth year (Draper and Sharp, 2006) found that two-thirds of these teachers reported that the McCrone obligations to engage in 35 hours of CPD represented no change for them, but there remained others who saw it as extra, as 'something else to fit in over and above work'. In addition, while many saw no change for themselves half believed it represented change for some of their colleagues, and a third for most or all of their colleagues. While formal and contractual expectations of teachers' work have changed and now incorporate CPD as an integral part, CPD is clearly currently not perceived by all teachers as a core part of their work.

Implications for induction

Induction may be understood as supportive and also as an educational experience, socialising new staff into the culture and expectations of the workplace as well as providing scope for development and collaboration. Ensuring the effectiveness of collaboration may, however, require training for those centrally involved. Mutual support may prove difficult for those at different stages of their professional development. Induction's current role in Scotland is perceived at least in part to be to establish professional development as an integral part of the work of teachers, an entitlement, an obligation and an expectation . . . a part of the psychological as well as the legal contract. Given this, the nature of induction would be expected to be developmental in itself. Induction activities should be learning activities, and to reflect understandings of what makes for good professional development. They should also take account of what the learner can contribute to the process, a collaborative rather than a didactic model, and of what the learner perceives to be needed; that is, new teachers should play a part in deciding what those activities shall be, in order that they can meet current needs. In the next chapter we shall explore current mechanisms for induction in Scotland and elsewhere, before moving on to consider its role for more experienced teachers changing job within teaching.

Chapter 3

POLICY AND PRACTICE IN INDUCTION FOR BEGINNING TEACHERS

In this chapter we review and contrast the experiences of new teachers and the systems in place for them in many parts of the developed world. The discussion leads to a set of key features of induction systems for new teachers. The needs of more experienced teachers will be revisited in Chapter 5.

Scotland

With the establishment of the General Teaching Council (GTC) in 1965, the Council became responsible for administering entry to the profession, through the provisional registration of beginning teachers, probationers, and, on their satisfactory completion of a two-year period of probation, their being given full membership of the profession. Prior to this, inspectors had judged the performance of new teachers. From 1965 teachers, as a self-regulating profession and through their professional body, took charge of the process of deciding who would be allowed to teach in Scotland's state schools.

Reports on probationer teachers and their teaching were written by headteachers and submitted to the Council at the end of the first year and at the end of the second year. Satisfactory teaching led to passing probation (often known as 'getting your parchment'); unsatisfactory teaching, or, unusually, unprofessional conduct would lead to either extended probation or withdrawal from the register. Only registered (or provisionally registered) teachers could teach in Scotland's publicly funded schools and probation was perceived as an opportunity to prove capability. Most new teachers passed probation without complication, but some failed to complete for a number of reasons: when or where work was scarce it was difficult for some to accrue the required number of days of teaching, some had little support and made little progress, some were not suited to full time work as a teacher although as students they might have performed well, some failed to meet unusually high standards, some were given classes other experienced teachers had found impossible. Support, advice, assistance and opportunities for development varied. The General Teaching Council for Scotland's own internal analysis (GTCS, 1990) suggested that procedures were not being consistently followed. A three-year national study of probationers (SOP) (Draper *et al.*, 1991) revealed difficulties and inconsistencies in practice in relation to the recruitment and employment of new teachers, and also in their induction, support and assessment. Some taught in the absence of information about school policies and procedures, feedback on teaching was sparse, support when offered was frequently not matched to current need, many probationers had observed no other teachers teaching and many were not clear whether their teaching was adequate until they saw the reports written about them at the end of the year. All was not well.

At the same time the concept of staff development was beginning to inform thinking and probation began to be seen as an opportunity for development, rather than simply for proving competence as a teacher. However lack of information on the practice and development of probationers meant that support, when offered, was often not targeted at current needs.

The SOP project suggested that not only did new teachers need support but those who supported them needed support themselves in order to carry out their role effectively. New materials were produced to support new teachers with areas that had been identified by the research as serially problematical for beginners, including class management and organisation, time management and identifying and meeting special needs. Materials were also published by the GTCS for schools: an initial booklet on assessing probationers was followed by videos and support materials. These focused on probation as a time for development as well as of assessment, and assessment itself was presented as a mechanism for identifying development needs and appropriate support.

A study some five years later which scrutinised the employment and support experiences of beginning teachers (Draper *et al.*, 1997b) found signs of improvement in the experience of some, but also established that only half of new teachers had the expected (and desirable) experience of stable employment in one school, which would enable meaningful identification of needs and targeted support. Many new teachers changed school more than once and a small but significant group struggled through their probationary period, making up the required 380 days in numerous schools with supply teaching (sometimes for just half a day). A further project explored the experiences of those who had succeeded in completing their probation 'on supply' (Draper *et al.*, 1998a). The worst example recorded was of one teacher who worked in 52 schools with over 120 separate periods of employment, which offered no hope for carefully assessed teaching or development needs and targeted support. These teachers had had plenty of practice in developing survival skills with new classes but little opportunity for working in the longer term or in depth with either pupils or colleagues. When it came to their assessment there was little evidence on their professional practice in any one school and it was clearly hard to be robust in judgements on their practice, after they had struggled to complete the required time. The GTCS established a working party to investigate the employment arrangements for probationers and condemned the employment of new teachers in such circumstances, while recognising that where jobs where scarce it might be the only way for new teachers to find opportunities to begin their careers.

Around that time, and against a background of teacher discontent about workload and the pace of development and educational initiatives, the McCrone Inquiry was set up to explore the situation (pay and conditions) of teachers. The subsequent report (SEED, 2000) and the Agreement which followed (SEED 2001) brought significant changes to teachers' work, including the incorporation of CPD as part of the job of every teacher in Scotland, an entitlement and an obligation. Probation came under strong scrutiny and the McCrone Report, like the GTCS, condemned the plight of probationers on supply as 'scandalous' and no way to begin a professional career, and a series of changes were agreed which radically altered the experiences of new teachers in Scotland (SEED 2001).

Probation was reduced to one year but a post for that period was guaranteed for all those qualifying as teachers in Scotland (from within the EU), signalling a commitment to reduce the angst associated with finding a first post. Guaranteed support would be provided by experienced teachers and those entering the profession would have a reduced workload, with a day and a half a week for preparation/assessment and professional development. There would be regular observations and feedback, and these would be focused not random or general. Finally, reflecting the development of a set of standards in Scotland and a career-long framework for CPD, a new standard, the standard for full registration (SfR) (GTCS, 2002a) would be the goal that all new teachers would have to meet by the end of their induction year. The new arrangements were introduced in August 2002 and several studies have explored their impact (Draper *et al.*, 2004; McNally, 2006).

Much of what was seen as inadequate has been overtaken to at least some extent by the new arrangements. Posts were found (with some difficulty) for all new teachers. Initial orientation to key policies and procedures, self-evaluation and feedback and the collection of evidence of competence against the Standard (SfR) are all part of the induction process. These repre-sent real progress in terms of developing a more satisfactory induction for new teachers. However there have also been concerns. Experience is still varied with, for example, some settings being more supportive than others, some new teachers receiving more easily their time out of class, variations in the number and style of observations. There is also a concern that the Standard itself and the induction process as a whole were somewhat instrumental and bureaucratic, with a focus on checking performance against the standard and completing the required paperwork rather than offering scope for individual need and development, creativity and innovation. Guaranteed support is clearly welcome. The concern is that it may serve to narrow expectations of both new teachers and their mentors and assessors, defining effective teaching and scaffolding a model for professional development which is constrained rather than open-ended.

High direction/high support: the Scottish induction arrangements

In terms of the model explored in Chapter 1, the current Scottish arrangements for the induction of beginner teachers would seem to fall into the high direction/high support quadrant. Is this unusual?

We shall seek to address this question in two ways: firstly by looking at a comparative study of induction in Hong Kong, and secondly by exploring some forms of induction from around the globe.

Comparing Scotland and Hong Kong

Findings on the early experiences of new secondary teachers in Scotland (Draper *et al.*, 2004) have been compared with the findings of a study of new teachers in Hong Kong. (Details of the Hong Kong study may be found in Forrester and Draper (2005).) New teachers in Hong Kong reported experiences that were in some ways similar to those which prevailed in Scotland prior to the introduction of the new induction scheme in 2002. They had to find their own posts and support was not formalised. Their situation was different, however, in that there was no probation period and no post-qualifying assessment of their competence as teachers. They were full teachers from the start.

The contrasting experiences of these two groups may be used to test out the model outlined in Chapter 1 and variations in the induction period can be mapped as in Figure 3.

Figure 3: Location of induction programmes on the proposed model

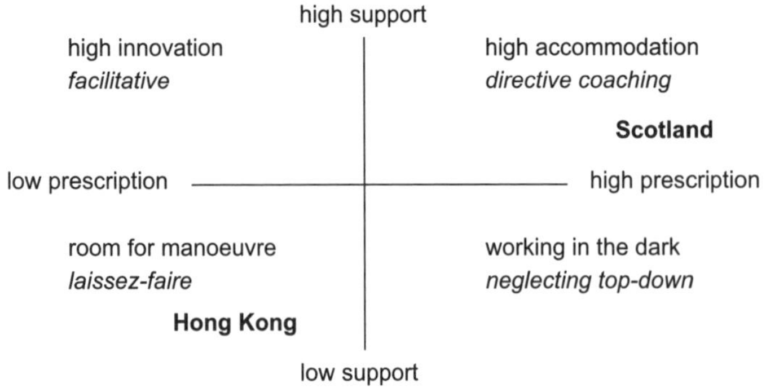

What kinds of experiences do these represent for new teachers?

For those located in the *directive coaching* quadrant, teachers received support to meet a predetermined outcome. For those who were supporting new teachers this enabled a programme of support to be built round identified end points. For the new teachers themselves there was a stronger focus on externally set outcomes and provision than there might have been otherwise, and their thinking about practice and their development was often infused and shaped by concerns over whether they were doing what others wanted and whether they were collecting the 'right' evidence. These characteristics can be seen as both strengths and weaknesses. The clarity of what is wanted may ensure that development opportunities are offered, rather than the complexity of new teachers' situations making suitable provision difficult to identity or of good intention being overwhelmed by alternative demands on resources. It may be more likely that support for new teachers will actually be resourced.

In contrast those in a *laissez-faire* system may find, as the Hong Kong teachers did, that there was little or no formal resourcing of support to meet their needs. They were freer to develop along their own chosen path but it was a lone path that they trod. They were free to go their own way and do more as they liked, but this threw them back on their own resources and professional judgement at an early stage, to do what they thought was best, but left them with little understanding of how well they were doing.

The two other quadrants logically follow from the modelling process. In a *neglecting top-down* situation, lacking both direction and support, new teachers would have to try to second guess how they were supposed to teach, and what was wanted of them. They would be concerned about whether they were getting it 'right'.

The facilitative quadrant is the direct opposite. The *facilitative* quadrant, like the directive coaching quadrant, assumes support as an entitlement. But here, unlike directive coaching, new teachers would be supported to develop their practice in ways they felt were right for them. They would have to spell out their needs in order to receive appropriate support and they would be more able to contribute to the design of a useful and individualised support system It is not inconceivable that this could operate within a broad conception of effective practice which still left room for some individuality, but examples appear to be lacking. The context in which induction schemes for new teachers have been developed has been characterised by a more managerial and centralised policy process that leads towards a more directive coaching system.

Induction practice in England

The policy for induction in England has many similar aspects to those in Scotland, although the timetable element is less reduced. The most recent research on induction in England (Bubb *et al.*, 2005; Bubb and Earley,

2006) while confirming that the new regulations are an improvement on the previous situation, offers a picture of gaps between policy and practice, between rhetoric and reality. While the English induction scheme may be seen to embody similar intentions to other modernised schemes of induction, and to lean more to the directive coaching style outlined above, recent findings on the induction experience reveal significant problems in implementing the policy. Bubb and Earley highlight significant gaps in implementation with regard to teachers receiving their entitlement of time out of class and support for their development. They highlight the complexity of effective induction and report widespread contraventions of the regulations. They attribute failure to implement fully the regulations to a number of sources including ignorance (and more rarely deliberate flouting) of the regulations, poor management in schools and inadequate monitoring by local education authorities. They track the consequences of under-resourcing and identify problems at policy, school and individual teacher levels. The ways in which experiences fall short of intention they call educational vandalism and see its inevitable results as unrealised teaching potential, the loss of good teachers and diminished student learning.

These data and those from Scotland reinforce the notion that even if a policy is in place that reflects both the needs of new staff and an understanding of what makes for effective professional development, *policies and their associated regulations can be no more effective than their implementation in practice.*

Induction arrangements: around the globe

In reviewing induction across the globe it appears as an idea whose time has come for many of those starting work as teachers, even if not for those changing jobs within teaching. In many parts of the developed world, induction is now a core part of the arrangements in place for beginning teachers. However there remains considerable diversity both in whether induction programmes exist and, if they do, in how they function. This chapter and Chapter 4 will explore the range of variation that exists with a view to drawing conclusions about elements which might form part of an effective induction programme in many contexts. There is inevitably much more information and analysis of programmes where induction is taken seriously, therefore the focus of this section will tend towards what looks promising in terms of induction practice rather than being a full account of the full range of experiences of beginning teachers.

The process of reviewing arrangements is made simpler by the existence of two quite comprehensive meta-analyses of induction: one by the Asia Pacific Economic Co-operation ministerial group (APEC) (1997), which focuses particularly on arrangements in New Zealand, Australia and Japan but also reports on Canada, Korea, Brunei Darussalam and Singapore, and one for the United States, compiled by the American Federation of Teachers (AFT) in 2001.

Key elements in induction programmes

The APEC study reviewed induction in eleven Pacific Rim economies and reported detailed case studies in three (Australia, New Zealand and Japan). They suggest that the following conditions are characteristic of 'promising' induction arrangements:

- a culture of shared responsibility, where all professionals take active roles in a new teacher's acculturation and transition;
- multiple support strategies used, including mentoring, modelling good practice, orientation/familiarisation, in-service training (professional development);
- a nurturing environment which is responsive to its context and to the needs of individual teachers;
- interaction of new and experienced teachers;
- a continuum of professional development;
- down-played assessment;
- clearly defined goals;
- adequate political, financial and time commitments.

The AFT review of induction in 50 states of the US, which reported in 2001, found that 34 (68 per cent) states had induction programmes for beginning teachers – up from 30 per cent in the 1980s (Hirsch *et al.*, 2001). In 22 of the 34 states induction was mandatory and funded. In consequence less than half of the states went beyond good intention to real provision and one third of states were 'silent on induction' (AFT, 2001, p. 4). Based on their evidence, the AFT review suggests the following are characteristics of effective induction:

- inclusion: induction for *all* new teachers irrespective of their entry route to teaching in order to ensure all teachers are given the best start to working in schools;
- duration: all induction to last at least one year;
- mentoring: all new teachers being assigned qualified mentors who are experienced teachers, and mentors are given time and recognition for the role;
- time for induction: new teachers being given reduced teaching loads;
- successful completion requires review of teaching: evidence of successful practice rather than of completing a period of time teaching.

There is considerable overlap in the findings of the two meta-analyses, although there is less in the AFT report on the process or culture of induction than in the earlier APEC study and a stronger focus on mechanisms, but the notion of inclusion adds an extra value dimension to the debate. If induction is perceived less as a luxury and more as a necessity for anyone to teach effectively in schools, it is logical that it should be offered to anyone entering teaching and indeed logical beyond that that it should operate for anyone moving into a school at any career stage. (This point is explored further in Chapter 5.)

Turning to an exploration of mechanisms of induction, the APEC study highlights the role of:

- mentoring;
- modelling good practice;
- targeted intervention;
- assessment.

AFT supports the provision of mentors and emphasises that mentors require time and support for their role as well as new teachers themselves. The study of probationers (SOP) (Draper *et al.*, 1991) also highlighted the demands of supporting new entrants and drew attention to the need for mentor training, as well as clarity in the mechanisms and personnel involved in formative and summative assessment.

There appears to be general agreement that some form of assessment / review of teaching / perusal of evidence is important to complete the process but its form and function is considered differently. APEC suggest that assessment should focus on development of skills in addition to informing certification. It argues that where certification is prominent this undermines its developmental value and reports that certification is not universal. It may be, however, that where certification is required, assessment inevitably takes on a 'proving' connotation.

Suggested future developments in induction

APEC identifies the following as needing further consideration:

- links between institutions where new teachers are initially trained (and educated);
- adequate amounts of school experience during initial preparation;
- continuity between initial preparation and induction;
- committed financial support for induction;
- equity across teachers in different sectors, phases and circumstances.

Reviewing the evidence above, it seems that there are significant differences in the *purposes, focus, design, management and process* of induction.

The purposes and goals of induction

A major emphasis in arguments in favour of induction is its impact on teacher *retention*. Global concerns about teacher supply may underpin the recent growth in interest in induction. Certainly strong claims are made about the effects of induction in retaining staff, especially in the US (Darling-Hammond, 1990; Johnson and Birkeland, 2003).

Smooth *transition* from pre-service training/education to working as a teacher is another overt purpose. Smoothness of transition is seen as desirable for new teachers but also, one would expect though this is not stated explicitly, for their charges. The 'reality shock' of the move into actual teaching is recognised and the need to ameliorate its effects as much as possible is seen as desirable. Continuity between pre-service programmes and teaching is thought to enable new teachers to draw upon their earlier learning rather than falling purely into survival mode and starting from scratch. Transitions are sent to be smoother with appropriate support and further opportunities for learning.

Some see a period of induction as an opportunity to test whether a teacher is 'up to the job', as an extended selection procedure where a teacher is on trial or probation. Others, reflecting a more lifelong learning approach, see it as a continuation of professional development from pre-service days and assume that this development will be helped by space, time and support to reduce the impact of the reality shock to enable an easing into full time working in teaching.

The focus of induction programmes

These differences in view about the purpose of induction inevitably lead to variations of focus in the programmes themselves. Some have as a key element the assessment of whether someone is a good enough teacher to continue in the profession and may reflect an assumption that some people are 'born teachers'. Such an approach could be argued to be in direct conflict with the more developmental assumption which has a stronger focus on induction as a developmental period: a time for learning and improving, rather than proving, and which assumes that people can learn to be teachers and can change how they teach through further learning. This latter assumption underpins the whole concept of professional development, and indeed without it there is little point in professional development. In practice, of course, even those taking a 'born teacher' position will usually concede that people can learn to change and improve their teaching, but the questions are then how long it would take for them to be able to teach at an acceptable level, and what would be the costs for pupils/students and in other staff time for the provision of support? Both of these underline the difference between a developmental and a proving focus.

Most induction programmes offered have an element of both proving and developing but it is the balance between these that varies significantly, leading to very different experiences for new teachers in the different settings. There are also other additional sources of variation.

A further dimension of focus concerns the extent to which induction is focused on the development of classroom practice or whether it also acknowledges the breadth of the teacher's role (including relationships with colleagues, parents, wider agencies and the community), the need for integration, both professional and social, and acculturation into the school as a community of practice, the potential for the new teacher to make a contribution to the school, the development of a professional identity and the role of work on the individual's life, that is, that teachers have a wider life and identity within which their work is located. As noted above, Goodson (1994) and others have bemoaned the tendency of modernisation initiatives to focus on teaching as technical and instrumental work, overlooking the more complex dimensions of the professional work of teachers.

A further aspect to consider is to what extent there is a recognition of the contribution that any new member of staff might make to the organisation, bringing views and experiences from elsewhere. As noted above, several headteachers, asked about their selection of staff (Draper *et al.*, 1997), reported that they liked to employ beginning teachers for a range of reasons which included their freshness of approach and new ideas. Induction should thus pave the way for all new members of staff to shape the organisation they join as well as being acculturated into it. For schools to operate as learning organisations, new questions and new ideas from other settings are valuable. Induction should therefore seek in part to identify strengths and experiences which a new member of staff brings. An effective selection process will have already identified some of these and plans can be made to make the most of them.

A final dimension of focus in induction is the extent to which the experience is fixed and how much it is shaped round the individual needs of the new member of staff. This balance is not as straightforward as it may appear. Where there is little flexibility about content, a comprehensive programme will ensure that key information on policies and procedures is given to everyone but the provision may be one of lowest common denominator with some staff being supported in ways they do not need, while other needs remain unmet. The danger of one size fits all is that what is done fits no one very well. Some tailoring and differentiation may therefore be helpful but it must be remembered that induction should be both protective and reasonably comprehensive. At the same time busy people in new jobs may need some support and information drip-fed over time; it is not helpful to be bombarded with information which cannot be retained. And, as with all learning, relevance is an important motivator, hence some information may be best acquired when actually needed.

The management of induction

A further dimension of variation arises in how individual programmes are managed: where the responsibility for the programmes lies and the extent to which they are resourced.

In some contexts induction is run from the centre, and managed at a national level (as is the case, for example, in Japan, Papua New Guinea and Taipei) by government or by a professional body or jointly. In others, responsibility lies more locally at local government level (as in Australia, Canada, the US and Korea) and managed across schools. In other contexts responsibility lies mainly with schools (for example, in New Zealand, Singapore and Brunei Darussalam). Differences flowing from these are multiple: programmes vary in their formality, in resourcing, in priority, in the degree to which they are contextualised to local and individual priorities and needs. In practice, of course, those programmes laid down centrally at national level are often implemented locally by local government or schools, with varying degrees of overlap.

A further variation arises in relation to whether there is post-qualifying certification of teachers or whether they are deemed to be fully qualified and full teachers at the end of their initial preparation and training. Where there is post-qualifying assessment this shapes induction as a hurdle to be overcome; where there is not, induction is more flavoured by the idea of 'settling in' or familiarisation, but is also generally less likely to attract resources. Expectations that CPD will be more than rhetoric and require to be resourced also vary between systems and shape expectations of the induction period. Professional bodies, where they exist as guardians of the profession and professional standards rather than as trade unions, are not all identical in their remits and play different roles within the systems. In Scotland, for example, the long-established General Teaching Council is central to the process and is involved in the allocation of new teachers to areas of the country and in the scrutiny of their professional development and achievement of the SfR as well as accrediting ITE and CPD. In England, in contrast, the Department for Education and Skills (DfES) is central to the induction process and the GTC becomes involved if teachers are deemed to have failed their induction, since the Council is the body to whom they submit an appeal.

The management of some induction arrangements includes the allocation of new teachers to training posts (for example, in Scotland) while in other contexts teachers find their own jobs and the induction programme then follows. In some contexts the jobs open to beginning teachers are temporary, for example, in Belgium (Kelchtermanns and Ballet, 2002). This militates against integrating into a school community, and is exacerbated if the job is part-time. The circumstance of beginning teaching in a temporary post has been found to have specific drawbacks (Draper *et al.*, 1997b) and was strongly criticised as unhelpful for professional integration and development

(McCrone Report: SEED, 2000). Around half of those who began teaching in Scotland in 1995 worked full time in one school while others worked part time or in several schools. Some had to complete their probation, at that time a two-year period, by teaching in a temporary capacity and accumulating experience in a large number of schools. This resulted in great uncertainty and an undermining of their self-confidence in their competence. They worried about immediate and future employment and received few, if any, opportunities for professional development. If they chose to stay in teaching, the average length of time it took them to complete the required number of days of teaching was three-and-a-half years (Draper *et al.*, 1997b; SEED, 2001). Being a beginning teacher on these temporary contracts led to an emphasis on coping, on quickly establishing short-term relationships with pupils and staff and on securing further employment (Draper *et al.*, 1997b), with professional development as a distant goal. Teachers who began work in such circumstances found themselves working in a diminished version of the teacher's role. They missed the opportunity that more settled work offers for building and sustaining supportive relationships with colleagues, developing and maintaining long-term relationships with pupils, and longer term preparation, planning and goal setting. They absorbed a limited view of the work of teaching and, faced with day-to-day survival in different schools, their expectations of professional development opportunities beyond survival were low.

As induction becomes more formalised more structure appears within the process. This may or may not be inevitable but it is certainly common. The structure commonly takes the form of a standard or sets of competencies (in Scotland called competences) that act as a guide to the development that is expected and should be supported during the induction period. It also serves to define the level to be reached by the end of induction. In some cases this expected standard of performance also becomes a definition for competence of experienced teachers. Again there are fears that, as with assessment, this diminishes the role of new teachers in shaping their induction since it offers a curriculum for induction which is essentially predetermined and this raises questions about the scope for innovative teaching and individualised programmes.

Induction also varies in the extent to which programmes are resourced and what that means in terms of provision . . . and therefore whether induction support is an entitlement or merely an aspiration. Where assessment is a requirement for post-qualification certification there is also the question of how the resource is split between tasks related to proving competence and time spent developing. This is particularly the case if assessment arrangements are cumbersome and bureaucratic and where considerable time may be absorbed by these processes. Where assessment is required, time must be spent on it to ensure membership of the profession and this brings its own priority. Given teacher time for development will always be limited, then time spent on proving inevitably reduces time spent on developing. It is arguable whether the process of assessment can also be part of development. Findings from new teachers (Draper *et al.*, 1991; Bubb *et al.*, 2005) suggest that assessment and development are perceived by some teachers at least as mutually exclusive processes and issues may not be raised with assessors if they are seen to undermine the likelihood of 'passing'. Indeed the micro-politics of the situation (Kelchtermanns and Ballet, 2002) may loom large. New teachers in Scotland (Draper *et al.*, 1991) spoke of seeking to manage impressions of their teaching competence using a range of strategies which included drawing attention to things that were going well.

The design of induction

The programmes themselves vary significantly. They are of differing duration from a few weeks or months to five years. They vary in their starting-point: some begin well ahead of actual appointment, while others begin when teaching begins. Some are predominantly individualised programmes, while others seek to bring new teachers together for sharing and joint development. Some offer mentoring and/or coaching, others do not. Some offer time out of class for preparation, observation of others teaching, visits to schools, attendance at courses. Some are funded to enable release of time from class responsibility for new teacher and/or mentor while others are not. There are variations in the role of assessment in induction, and who assesses, and in the clarity and transparency of criteria and methods used in assessment. Where programmes have been funded there appears to be considerable pressure to reduce costs with some programmes being cut back or terminated. This suggests that commitment to induction is not guaranteed, and that induction itself may be regarded as a luxury rather than an essential part of supporting teachers in new posts, or a fashionable initiative which will soon be replaced by another. Given the evidence of its impact it would be hoped that it would become part of standard policy for teachers but fears, voiced by APEC, raise concern about long-term practice. The AFT (US) study concludes firmly that 'Support and assistance in the initial years of teaching produces teachers who are better equipped for the challenges of the classroom, have a greater likelihood of becoming high quality teachers and are more likely to remain in the profession. Induction programs represent a good investment, one that is likely to pay dividends for students far into the future' (AFT, 2001, p. 6).

The process of induction

The process refers to the tone or nature of the relationships which operate within the induction programme itself, that is, the extent to which the environment is nurturing, the extent to which the inductee's strengths and experience are seen as a source of potential contribution (rather than solely as deficient) and the extent to which induction is seen as a joint and shared enterprise between inductors and inductee, indicated in part by scope for the new teacher to influence the shape of the programme. The Scottish experience of induction suggests that treatment of new teachers reflects the prevailing style of human resource management of teachers in the system.

A key element of the process of induction is understood to be the relationship of the new teacher with their key supporter(s), often referred to as mentoring. Clutterbuck (2001) has suggested that mentoring 'is a means of assisting transitions in thinking patterns', that an important aspect of mentoring is the degree of formality in mentoring arrangements and in the interactions and relationships involved, and that mentoring contributes significantly to the speed with which satisfactory induction ('settling in') is achieved.

The next chapter explores issues of focus, process and design in more detail, with a particular emphasis on the role of standards and the processes of mentoring and coaching. In Chapter 5 we explore the induction offered to more experienced teachers changing post or school and will draw again on the five headings which have emerged here: the *purposes, focus, design, management and process* of induction

Postscript: beyond the induction of beginning teachers

Systems vary in the provision they make for post-induction professional development. Some treat the first three or five years in teaching as a unit, seeking to ensure continuity from ITE/ITT to induction and on into the transition between induction and post induction, to keep the ball rolling on CPD. Others focus attention on the induction year and then teachers are left to sink or swim. In some systems there is career progression in the set of posts and opportunities for which they now become eligible, while for others there is a flat plain before the next steps on the professional development and career ladders become approachable.

Findings on good practice in induction emphasise the value of continuity, of support and feedback and of good provision of CPD opportunities. Designing development systems which operate in the years immediately after initial induction is likely to support an expectation in teachers that CPD is part of the job and is also likely to reinforce intentions to remain in teaching . . . to act, in effect, as an inoculation against leaving. However, there is a dilemma. The more resources are put into an initial induction year the more difficult it will be to sustain that in subsequent years. The more new teachers learn CPD is part of the job the more they are likely to be stressed or disappointed as higher workload kicks in, making it more difficult to sustain CPD activities. Reshaping initial induction may generate expectations and appetites that are difficult to satisfy!

Chapter 4

INDUCTION: STANDARDS AND SUPPORT STRUCTURES

In Chapter 2, we discussed a range of policy initiatives and analysed several models of professional development and their varied contribution to teacher growth, confidence and effectiveness. In this chapter we turn to consider the detail of the teacher standards and structural approaches adopted in various countries when they consider what requires to be put in place to support new teachers. How more experienced teachers taking on new and specific roles and functions such as headship or principalship are supported and inducted is considered in Chapter 5.

Standards

Teacher standards associated with perceived stages of teacher development such as the induction phase or for 'expert' teacher status have appeared in many countries, for example, New Zealand (Ministry of Education, 1999), within the US both at state level, for example, Washington (2005), or nationally though National Boards (National Board of Professional Teaching Standards, 2002; Serafini, 2005), and similarly at national level in Australia with the publication of *A National Framework for Professional Standards for Teaching* (Ministerial Council on Education, Employment Training and Youth Affairs, 2003) or in certain states within Australia (Brock, 2002; Victorian Institute of Teaching, 2003). While there have been important initiatives driven by professional bodies such as the National Council of Teachers of Mathematics (1991) in the US, the majority of professional standards have been introduced as part of various governments' beliefs and related strategies for developing and maintaining high quality teaching and leadership in schools and improving learning outcomes for pupils. The reasons for government involvement vary, but according to Ingvarson (1998, p. 3),

> the [teaching] profession has yet to build its own infrastructure for defining high quality teaching standards, promoting development towards those standards and providing recognition for those who reach them; in other words, teaching has yet to build a professional development system based on profession-defined teaching standards . . .

Those standards which have materialised have not overtly been imposed, as many have been the subject of consultation and agreements between governments, teacher unions and other representative bodies, but there have been academic concerns about standards as being too technicist, atomistic, forcing conformity, disavowing experimentation and spontaneity and leaving little scope for the individual teacher to exercise professional judgement. Wilkin (1999, Section 1) in a discussion of teacher preparation in England suggests:

> Teacher training has become painting by numbers, or rather learning to teach by numbers; and, moreover, institutions are to be checked to see whether they are painting carefully and accurately within the lines.

Concerns about de-professionalising teaching and the production of teachers as mere technicians have manifested themselves in a number of countries, not least in parts of the US where there are fears that local teaching cultures and partnerships are subsumed within technical-rationalist-behaviourist approaches demanded by the standards initiative.

There are claims that the national standards movement is intent on spelling out the forms of knowledge, dispositions and extent of performance that teachers are to adhere too, and that:

> Among the most disheartening of the emerging results of this direction is a narrowing of what counts as quality and accountability in teacher education, and an equally problematic perspective concerning the means that will accomplish the ends being promoted. At the core of this agenda is a politically enticing but conceptually misplaced view of teaching and schooling that hearkens back to earlier eras, when a search for certainty and predictability was mounted that, it was hoped, would guarantee particular classroom outcomes related to what is termed 'learning'. (Beyer, 2002, p. 240)

This mirrors concerns about 'restricted' and 'extended' professionality first raised by Hoyle (1969) and which is concerned with the knowledge, skills and processes employed by teaching professionals.

While many of the emerging standards are 'intended to help teachers to recognise their professional strengths, identify learning and development goals and devise plans to meet those goals' (State of Queensland, 2005, p. 4), thus supporting the concept of professional reflection and subsequent action, there is a growing move for such standards to be aligned with various forms of performance management and appraisal and pay as in New Zealand and England. Standards may be viewed therefore alternatively as controlling, gate-keeping devices or as supportive tools and instruments that encourage teachers to identify strengths and weaknesses or in softer or developmental terms – areas for further development. In various jurisdictions, the standards are claimed to demonstrate an on-going political commitment 'to ensuring that students have the opportunity to learn from, and that schools are managed and led by, high quality professionals' (Ministry of Education: New Zealand, 1999, p. 5).

Scotland has developed its own Professional Development Framework of Standards (Table 1) that has emerged in a haphazard way since the early 1990s (Christie and O'Brien, 2005). While the actual development of the Framework was relatively unplanned and non-sequential and can be fairly described as 'piecemeal', there are obvious linkages between its elements that reflect stages of teacher development, namely, an Induction Standard (O'Brien and Christie, 2005); an 'expert' teacher standard – Chartered Teacher (Kirk *et al.*, 2003); a revised Standard for Headship (O'Brien and Torrance, 2005); all apparently building on the existing Standard or Benchmarks for ITE (Quality Assurance Agency for Higher Education [QAAHE], 2000). Since 2000, teacher standards policy development and associated structures in Scotland have been influenced by other events including the attempt to re-professionalise and re-culture the teaching profession in the light of the Teachers' Agreement (SEED, 2001) after the McCrone Inquiry. For example, as we have noted above, the McCrone Report described the then probationary period as disgraceful and recommended a period of 'stable employment' for Newly Qualified Teachers (NQTs), with guaranteed improved induction support (Draper *et al.*, 2004).

The development of teacher standards in Scotland has been led by government in a variety of guises and influenced by Her Majesty's Inspectorate of Education (HMIE) and civil servants within the governmental department of education. The Chartered Teacher Standard was developed by a project team that engaged in possibly the largest and most comprehensive educational consultation that the country has seen (Kirk *et al.*, 2003), but despite this was still subject to concerns about close government control (Purdon, 2003a; 2003b; 2004). The revised Standard for Headship (SEED, 2005) was, after consultation with stakeholders including the profession, employers and the higher education sector, the product of an *ad hoc* committee of interested / expert individuals / civil servants and officials such as the new National CPD Co-ordinator. The GTCS was charged by SEED with developing the Induction Standard as a joint project with a national development officer. The Standard for Full Registration (SfR) (GTCS, 2002), which underpins the new induction arrangements established by GTCS, reflected the work of the national induction project and discussions within Council and consultation with HMIE and SEED officials. McNally (2002, p. 160), the national development officer, is clear about the nature of such consultation and the control of the outcome of the SfR, stating clearly that the SfR project itself was driven by an official imperative to build a

Table 1: The Scottish Teacher Standards Framework – development timeline

Date	Stage	Standard or Official Publication
1993	Initial Teacher Education	*Guidelines for Teacher Training Courses* (SOED, 1993)
1998	Initial Teacher Education	*Guidelines for Initial Teacher Education Courses in Scotland* (SOEID, 1998a)
1998	Headship	*Standard for Headship* (SOEID, 1998b)
2000	Initial Teacher Education	*The Standard for Initial Teacher Education in Scotland* (QAAHE, 2000)
2002	Teacher Induction	*Standard for Full Registration* (GTCS, 2002)
2002	'Expert' or Chartered Teacher	*Standard for Chartered Teacher* (SEED, 2002)
2003	School Leadership Framework	*Continuing Professional Development for Educational Leaders* (SEED, 2003)
2005	Headship	*Ambitious Excellent Schools: The Standard for Headship* (SEED, 2005)

near replica of the ITE benchmarking standard (Quality Assurance Agency for Higher Education, 2000) and brooked practically no alternative to a competence-based view of professional practice.

If McNally's interpretation of events is accurate, and there is no reason to think otherwise, strict central governmental control is evident. The GTCS, however, as the principal professional body of the Scottish teaching profession complied with this and has subsequently endorsed other Standards in the framework. Purdon (2003a; 2003b; 2004) has suggested that the Standards Framework adopted in Scotland permits closer political control over the professional lives of teachers. Teachers, however, have accepted the SfR despite its complexities and other standards, because the overall approach to standards in Scotland has been promoted as a common-sense codification of teacher skills and abilities. An examination of any of the Scottish standards will illustrate that they assiduously attempt to avoid the 'technicist' approach favoured by the Teacher Training Agency in England. How does the SfR differ from other induction standards for new teachers?

The nature of induction standards

Standards for the induction of new teachers are becoming more common because, as we have noted, there is a genuine concern about the recruitment and retention of teachers and a recognition that 'getting a good start' is important in any new occupation but particularly in teaching. Effective and supportive beginnings and associated processes and structures now have a central role, while also in several systems acting as a quality threshold through formal assessment of the beginning teacher against the standard.

This is true of the Scottish approach and we discuss the assessment role in more detail below.

The Scottish Induction Standard (SfR)

The SfR 'sets out clearly what is expected of new teachers during their induction process and provides a professional standard against which decisions will be taken on full registration' (Robson and Pearson, 2004, p. 1). This is clearly demonstrated in the Standard (GTCS, 2002, p. 3) itself where the twin purposes of the standard are set out, establishing descriptors of the professional qualities and capabilities that NQTs are expected to develop in the induction year and providing a set of competences against which the inductee will be assessed during that period to determine their suitability for full registration with the GTCS, without which they cannot teach in state schools in Scotland.

There are three interrelated categories in the SfR, building deliberately on existing ITE standards or benchmarks (QAAHE, 2000):

- professional knowledge and understanding;
- professional skills and abilities;
- professional values and personal commitment;

and inductees are expected to consolidate in certain areas while extending their skills and abilities in others.

These categories are subject to further division, with the competences expected outlined and illustrations of pertinent practice provided. The following Tables provide some limited illustration of this, while a complete picture can be obtained from the Appendix in the SfR (GTCS, 2002) or by reviewing additional material on the GTCS website (http://www.gtcs.org.uk/web/site/Home/home.asp) where, interestingly, the new induction process is still referred to as probation, perhaps stressing the assessment role more than the developmental role associated with induction?

McNally, the national development officer, has indicated that an opportunity was lost in the Scottish induction project. As we have noted, there was a political imperative associated with a competence-focused standard being developed and the opportunity to engage in review and debate about alternatives was not taken up. McNally (2002, p. 152) again does not shirk from indicating why this might be:

> … an absence of dialogue with the critical face of HE has characterised the policy making establishment within Scotland for more than a decade . . . Even a willingness to engage with some of the softer extant ideas in the literature has been absent. If not actually suppressed such input was not encouraged. As a result, potentially useful models of teacher development . . . did not inform initial thinking on the national project on professional development for teachers.

Table 2: An illustration of SfR structure and competences relating to professional knowledge and understanding

Professional knowledge and understanding		
Sub-category	**Competence**	**Illustration of professional practice**
Curriculum	Registered teachers have detailed knowledge and understanding of the relevant areas of the pre-school, primary or secondary school curriculum.	understand how to match the level of the curriculum area or subject(s) to be taught to needs of pupils use and adapt materials for learning and teaching which stimulate and challenge pupils
Education systems and professional responsibilities	Registered teachers have detailed working knowledge of their sector, of the school(s) in which they teach, and of their professional responsibilities within them.	have knowledge of the role and organisation of their employing authority, its policies and development priorities have working knowledge and understanding of the organisation and management of their school(s), including: school development planning; procedures for staff development and review; quality assurance and school improvement; and the relationship of these features to their responsibilities for classroom learning and teaching
Principles and Perspectives	Registered teachers can articulate their professional values and practices and relate them to theoretical principles and perspectives.	have knowledge and understanding of the stages of child development which they are able to use to take account of their pupils' needs have knowledge and understanding of the main theories of learning and draw on these in thinking about and planning their own teaching and pupils' learning

If this is the case and opportunities were lost, how does the SfR compare with standards and associated arrangements in other systems?

Induction Standards in England

The most obvious point of comparison would be with England, which in 1999 re-introduced a statutory induction process for NQTs through the Teacher Training Agency (TTA) (TTA, 1999a; Tickle, 2000b). The 1991 abolition of the probationary year was overturned by the Teaching and Higher Education Act 1998. The Act provided for the introduction of *Induction Standards*, allied to requirements to monitor the performance of new teachers, administer associated assessment procedures and the possible de-registration of individuals at the end of their first year. As in Scotland, the NQTs must work towards meeting the Induction Standards – a series of

Table 3: An illustration of SfR structure and competences relating to professional skills and abilities

Professional skills and abilities		
Sub-category	**Competence**	**Illustration of professional practice**
Teaching and learning	Registered teachers are able to plan coherent and progressive teaching programmes which match their pupils' needs and abilities, and they can justify what they teach.	have knowledge and understanding to justify the content and style of their teaching in terms of its value in the curriculum, its contribution to children's learning and general development, and its relevance to the needs of the pupils being taught
Classroom organisation and management	Registered teachers manage pupil behaviour and classroom incidents fairly, sensitively and consistently, making sensible use of rewards and sanctions, and seeking and using the advice of colleagues when necessary.	can use, in a consistent way, a variety of techniques to encourage pupils, promote positive behaviour and celebrate success seek and use advice from colleagues and promoted staff in managing more serious acts of indiscipline
Assessment of pupils	Registered teachers understand and apply the principles of assessment, recording and reporting.	can apply baseline, summative, and formative assessment, criterion and norm referenced techniques to assess pupils' attainments and monitor progress
Professional reflection and communication	Registered teachers convey an understanding of practice and general educational matters in their professional dialogue and communication.	possess, in discussion of educational matters, an understanding of the important issues

competence statements first issued in 1999, with the addition in 2001 of a requirement to pass the national numeracy test for teacher training candidates (TTA, 2001), while slightly modified Standards were issued in 2003 (TTA, 2003a). The English Induction Standards were one of a series of guidelines that made up a suite of documents covering:

- Standards for Qualified Teacher Status (TTA, 2003b);
- Special Educational Needs Co-ordinators (TTA, 1998a);
- Special Educational Needs Specialists (TTA, 1999b);
- Subject Leaders (TTA, 1998b); and
- Headteachers (DfES, 2000)

and clearly indicating that the competence movement had taken control of official thinking within the DfES and the TTA.

Table 4: An illustration of SfR structure and competences relating to professional values and personal commitment

Professional values and personal commitment		
	Competence	**Illustration of professional practice**
	Registered teachers show in their day-to-day practice a commitment to social justice and inclusion.	respect and value children and young people as unique, whole individuals value and promote fairness and justice and adopt anti-discriminatory practices in all regards, including gender, sexual orientation, race, disability, age, religion, culture and socio-economic background
	Registered teachers take responsibility for their professional learning and development	show a commitment to self-evaluation and continuing professional development as key means to improving practice and widening areas of expertise
	Registered teachers value, respect and are active partners in the communities in which they work	have positive relationships and partnerships within the community – with professional colleagues, with other professions, with parents, with other agencies and with the learners themselves can work co-operatively with other professionals recognising their different skills and possible different value bases

The current version of the Induction Standards in England located on the Training and Development Agency (TDA) [successor to the TTA] website (http://www.tda.gov.uk) have similar categories such as Professional values and practice; Knowledge and understanding; Teaching. The TDA advises NQTs that 'In your first three terms as a teacher, you can expect a tailored programme of training and support designed to equip you for the classroom and lay the foundations for your future professional development.' The Induction Standards make explicit the link to the standards for the award of Qualified Teacher Status (QTS). While there are six Induction Standards to overtake to complete the induction period satisfactorily, a NQT must also 'continue to meet the standards for the award of QTS, consistently and with increasing professional competence' (TTA, 2003a, p. 1). The Induction Standards reflect a view of teaching that is primarily concerned with classroom performance and pupil attainment and lays less stress on whole school/community issues and professional consideration of problematic issues than the Scottish SfR does where the broader role of the teacher is recognised more. Central control is evident in the English Standards where, for example, the 'secure knowledge and understanding' required is defined in the standard for the award of QTS in terms of the relevant stages of the National Curriculum Programme, National Numeracy and Literacy Strategies, and Key Skills as specified by the Qualifications and Curriculum Authority. As in Scotland, beginning teachers have their progress assessed and documented regularly and anyone who does not satisfy the Induction Standards within the allotted timeframe is ineligible for continuing employment as a teacher. Tickle (2000b, p. 705) expresses his disquiet and suggests:

> This reintroduction of the assessment of performance in core classroom practices, coupled with 'rigorous' assessment, and an emphasis on reporting procedures, seems to be symptomatic of a surveillance disposition attached to teacher education reforms in recent times.

Of course, one of the purposes of induction is to ensure that candidates satisfy the requisite standard, but if the standard is narrowly focused and if those engaged in the assessment have little experience of or sympathy with the notion of standards then there exists the danger of new teachers working towards meeting the requirements of their assessors only, which may involve an even more narrow range of classroom behaviours. The novice technician model may be reified by the process of assessment. Notions of the teacher as researcher, for example, are at odds with the views and declared experience of many existing school practitioners and beginning teachers may never 'experiment' or research their practice beyond fairly narrow boundaries and, as Chubbuck *et al.* (2001) suggest, may play along and play it safe.

Induction standards in other systems

In Australia, in the State of Victoria, the recently established Victorian Institute of Teaching (VIT) (which registers all teachers wishing to practice in the state's schools) established a 'Standards and Professional Learning Project' in 2003. A year-long induction programme was trialled; this involved a focus on the standards of professional practice (VIT, 2003) and incorporated mentor support. The Institute, in their Guide (VIT, 2004, p. 3), describes the purpose of the induction standards as follows:

> The Standards of Professional Practice for Full Registration provide teachers with a shared understanding of what the profession believes a teacher should know and be able to do. They also provide a basis for the collegial discussion and collaboration in teaching practice that underpins effective induction and mentoring programs.

Yet again we have a dual purpose of assuring the quality of teaching combined with the opportunities for professional learning. The VIT claims that these are interdependent and complementary.

The VIT standards comprise a 'Statement of Principle' plus eight standards grouped under the three 'themes' of: 'professional knowledge', 'professional practice' and 'professional engagement'. Each of the eight standards is further developed by four 'characteristics' of teaching. The Victorian standards (VIT, 2003) thus encompass:

- *Professional knowledge*
  - Teachers know how students learn and how to teach them effectively.
  - Teachers know the content they teach.
  - Teachers know their students.
- *Professional practice*
  - Teachers plan and assess for effective learning.
  - Teachers create and maintain safe and challenging learning environments.
  - Teachers use a range of teaching practices and resources to engage students in effective learning.
- *Professional engagement*
  - Teachers reflect on, evaluate and improve their professional knowledge and practice.
  - Teachers are active members of their profession.

The Australian Council for Educational Research (ACER) provided a team who evaluated (ACER, 2004) the development phase of the Victorian standards and support arrangements. The support provided included focused mentoring and involved a comprehensive training provision. The ACER report confirms the development of structured tasks for completion during the induction period, such as the Student Work Based Portfolio Task (SWBPT) and the classroom observations task involving new teacher and mentor in professional collaboration. These are part of the structured learning programme for beginning teachers but the tasks also provide materials for the portfolio, which would be the focus of professional dialogue and assessment by a Panel to assess in summative fashion whether the teacher should become fully registered by the VIT. The evaluators provided comments (ACER, 2004, pp. 9–10) such as:

> This was a wonderful learning tool for me. It helped me to understand the CSF learning outcomes and the different learning styles of the students. It was all about positive attitudes. My mentor worked with me every day and I had lots of informal chats with the principal as well as the more formal ones. (Graduate)

There was data familiar to Scottish researchers too:

> Only 50 per cent of graduates surveyed said that, in the classroom observation task, the mentors used the standards to give feedback.

> In the interviews, most of the mentors said that, in giving feedback to the graduates, they had drawn more on their own experiences of what 'worked' rather than the standards.

The Victorian experience suggests that structure is critical to supporting new teachers in their professional development and to allowing them to grow and to satisfy the pertinent standards in a productive way. How do other systems provide such structures of support?

Support structures

Draper *et al.* (2004, pp. 203–4) indicate that research during the last two decades on probation/induction raises a number of specific issues:

- Probationers had very different experiences in employment, support and assessment. Their experiences varied in amount and quality with some having much more developmentally oriented experiences than others.

- Probationers did not begin teaching at identical levels of skill and understanding in relation to teaching: their capacity to cope and their needs for support therefore varied. They also developed at different rates, partly as a consequence of different employment contracts and differing experiences of support assessment and feedback. A single model for probationer support was unlikely, therefore, to meet the needs of all beginning teachers.

- Probationers valued a range of support in type and source: both formal and informal support from both experienced and senior members of the profession and also from beginning teachers like themselves. The provision of effective support is thus complex.

So what is the nature of the structured support provided in various systems, how is it provided and what tensions exist with associated assessment regimes?

In England, DfEE Circular 5/99 set out the expectations associated with the reintroduction of an induction year for all new teachers in England and Wales. The Circular outlined responsibilities for mentors, employers and headteachers and established the elements of the Induction Year to include an entitlement to an individualised induction programme for each NQT, a 90 per cent teaching load, a Career Entry Profile as starting-point for development, observation, Professional Review of Progress, at least three summative assessment meetings during the year and a designated professional tutor or mentor (Barrington, 2000). Totterdell *et al.* (2002) provided an evaluation report on the new induction arrangements for the DfES. Their report suggests that much had been affirmed or improved in terms of structural support for beginning teachers but much improvement was also necessary. Worryingly among their findings was some disturbing data suggesting variability in the system and that a significant minority of NQTs were not receiving full support from their school or local educational authority. For example, while the 10 per cent reduced teaching timetable was considered a vital component of induction provision by all respondents, the surveys of NQTs showed that 20 per cent of the 1999–2000 cohort and 19 per cent of the 2000–1 cohort did not consistently receive this entitlement.

Tickle (2000a; 2000b), is highly critical of the arrangements in England and Wales, suggesting that it has all to do with the assessment and monitoring of probation and little to do with genuine induction practices and that an educational opportunity had been lost yet again.

In the US, as we noted in Chapter 3, the American Federation of Teachers produced an analysis (2001) of induction practices that demonstrated a growing state awareness of the importance of induction. Their evidence indicated that 22 states had funded and 'mandated' induction programmes for which successful completion resulted in a licence to be a teacher. There appears to be little consistency however among these programmes, some providing reduced workloads and release time for professional development opportunities while others do not do so.

Many individual states have initiated induction programmes in response to major concerns about the recruitment and retention of new teachers. As in the UK, there is potential for a crisis of supply of new teachers in the next few years as many teachers approach retirement age. Connecticut's Beginning Educator Support and Training (BEST) programme is described by Youngs (2003, p. 4), who indicates:

> Connecticut's approach to new teacher induction and assessment is designed to help novices learn to examine student learning, construct and apply subject-specific instructional knowledge, and reflect on their practice. While the state influences beginning teachers' induction experiences by training mentors, offering subject-specific seminars, and requiring second-year teachers to go through the high-stakes portfolio process, new teachers' experiences are also shaped by district policy related to induction. By supplementing the BEST program with a comprehensive array of support activities, a number of districts in Connecticut have fostered high levels of instructional quality.

The state had already been instrumental in co-operating with others through the Interstate New Teachers Assessment and Support Consortium (INTASC) to develop assessment standards in several content areas for the purpose of licensing teachers. An important emphasis in the Connecticut

BEST programme is subject-specific mentoring. Mentors are trained in a range of issues associated with mentoring 'including the needs of beginning teachers, the Connecticut teaching standards, and the BEST portfolio requirements. Participants discuss strategies for establishing trust, instructional coaching, promoting reflective inquiry, relating instructional practice to the teaching standards, and providing portfolio-related support' (Youngs, 2003, p. 10). Overall the emphasis in Connecticut appears to relate to a narrow band of 'instructional delivery', 'student assessment' and 'classroom management'.

In another New England state, the Massachusetts Department of Education provides a comprehensive website (www.doe.mass.edu/eq/mentor/teachers.html) that focuses on what they do in relation to induction which they view as not just about beginning teachers. This programme involves initial orientation; for beginning teachers, assignment to a mentor within their first two weeks; assignment to a support team and release time for mentors and the beginning teacher for classroom observation and other mentor-related activities.

The New Teacher Center at the University of Santa Cruz in California (www.newteachercenter.org/ti_scsvntp.php) has recently received attention in Scotland as its founders have been the guests of the Scottish Executive and are to be involved in providing further mentor training here; the Centre assists and supports new teachers entering the teaching profession and seeks to advance their skills and knowledge in relation to the California Standards for the Teaching Profession (CSTP). The Centre's website provides a range of information about their work in other US states.

What of our own Scottish approach? Previously we indicated that the long-established two-year induction period had become a fragmented and destabilising experience for many probationers, with little in the way of planned and sustained support. McNally's research (2002, p. 150) indicated a number of possible reasons for this:

> . . . the falling school rolls of the mid 1970s, followed by a tough economic climate; the right to supply cover in the teachers' contract of the mid 1980s; rights of supply teachers within employment legislation; delegation of management of staffing to schools; two reorganisations of local government; teacher surplus and shortage. The effect of these was that vulnerable new teachers became increasingly used for short-term supply work . . .

The SfR (GTCS, 2002) is the keystone of the new one-year induction period that replaced the outmoded and 'tired' probationary arrangements in 2002. Additionally, resources were provided to educational authorities and schools to pay for teacher participation in the new Induction Scheme, about which there was very little consultation and a hasty implementation. For an NQT, the Teacher Induction Scheme includes the guarantee of a year's placement in one or two schools, a reduced teaching load (70 per cent) and the support of a more senior member of staff as a mentor or 'supporter'. The remaining 30 per cent of the inductee's time is designated for development activities, again reflecting the central role played by CPD in the Agreement that followed the McCrone Report. Higher Education has been marginalised in the Induction Scheme despite currently having a major role in the other Standards within the Professional Development Framework, where partnership between the profession, the employers and Higher Education Institutions (HEIs) has been a condition of involvement and has been officially endorsed in numerous documents and statements by the SEED and the GTCS.

The educational authorities and schools have responded with varying degrees of success to the challenges the new Induction Scheme provides. A typical educational authority approach might be that adopted by Angus in the north-east of Scotland, which in June 2002 revised its guidance for schools and the new 'inductees'. The educational authority's amended guidance emphasised several new and important aspects of trainee support:

- School-based trainee support programmes should be based on a process of supported self-evaluation against *The Standard For Full Registration* (GTCS, 2002). The starting-point of this process should be the trainee teacher's Initial Teacher Education (ITE) 'Probationer File'.
- Trainee teachers are now entitled to participate in a planned programme of shadowing, observing and team teaching. The purposes of these activities should be identified beforehand through the process of supported self-evaluation, and follow-up discussion and action planning should take place.
- A centrally provided staff development programme will focus on key aspects of *The Standard for Full Registration* (SfR) and will complement school-based programmes.
- Each trainee teacher is required to maintain a folio containing a record of all staff development activities undertaken and of the outcomes of self-evaluation. This 'profile' will be included in an interim report to the GTCS in December and in the final report in June.

(Angus Council, 2002, Section 1)

The Angus documentation offers advice on the role and responsibilities of the headteacher especially with regard to final assessment and reporting which will result in full registration; advises on the role of the mentor – a theme expanded below – and includes a series of Appendices that provide checklists designed to support the initial induction process including consideration of key information and meetings at the beginning of the period of induction, plus providing self-evaluation 'tools' and a structure for subsequent meetings between mentor / supporter and the 'inductee'. Our survey of educational authorities' Induction Co-ordinators (Christie *et al.*, 2003) confirmed that similar information and advice was available from most educational authorities who took their new-found responsibilities seriously, however as the GTCS (Pearson and Robson, 2005, section 2.4.4) evidence below suggests, there are parts of the country who provide better structures and support than others.

Much of the research on the Scottish induction scheme since 2002 has focused on expectations of ITE students about to embark on the new induction scheme and what their fears and hopes were (Rippon and Martin, 2003; 2006). As noted above, research (Christie *et al.*, 2003) into the initial year of the new induction scheme involved a survey of educational authority co-ordinators and a series of case studies in secondary schools, this provided interesting evidence about the experience of the first year of the new scheme and some of the data has been confirmed by the annual collection and analysis of data and statistics associated with the induction scheme, undertaken by the GTCS. The Council has shared some of its evidence in a series of published reports based on surveys conducted. With regard to CPD, some of the issues raised by induction respondents (Pearson and Robson, 2005, section 2.4.4) are illuminating:

- most local authority CPD was of variable quality;
- much of the local authority CPD seemed to be a repeat of content previously covered in ITE where the input had often been of a higher quality;
- the SfR was often used as the framework for local authority CPD but was not a tool recognised by most schools.

While the potential of this early CPD entitlement is perhaps not yet realised, a possible outcome may be the desire of those satisfying the SfR to continue to seek out and engage with quality CPD activities as their needs change with experience. Certainly research into the first year of the induction scheme (Christie *et al.*, 2003) indicated a minimal use of the SfR in both developmental and assessment terms – there are echoes of this in the VIT experience summarised above. There was generally an ignorance around the case study schools about the nature and specifics of the SfR. Clearly there is a need for an independent evaluation of the Scheme or research into various aspects such as how the Standard is used and understood. The Economic and Social Research Council (ESRC) Project (McNally *et al.*, 2003) on early professional development not due to report till 2008 may offer critical insights into how new professionals actually learn and the role of standards in promoting or otherwise such learning. It would be useful subsequently to assess the Scottish induction scheme against the evidence and conclusions yet to be produced by McNally and his colleagues.

The induction scheme has been criticised for its hasty implementation and inadequate consultation (O'Brien and Christie, 2005; Purdon, 2003a). Indeed Draper *et al.* (2004) suggest there is evidence from the first year of the scheme in secondary schools that many supporter teachers had not even read the SfR and were blissfully unaware of the nature of the competences they were assessing, formally reporting on and using to discuss the inductee's developing CPD agenda. A major finding (O'Brien and Christie, 2005, p. 200), and of concern for the associated ongoing nature of teacher CPD in Scotland, was the 'absence of *conceptualising* or *reflective practice* from teachers' vocabulary' and the

> evidence that most instructional support of probationers is at the level of practical craft knowledge which does not go beyond 'what works'. There is a danger that, as supporters develop probationers within a fairly narrow range of classroom practice and probationers, in turn, strive to please their supporter-assessor, current practice will stagnate.

Clearly there is scope for interpretation of purpose associated with the development of the Scottish Standards Framework, for example, the Induction Standard, like those of other systems, and associated processes involve both support and formal summative assessment by the same person; it is about development surely but are there also elements which may be designed to secure conformity or maintain what exists rather than invite experimentation and encourage a degree of supported risk-taking? In relation to support, how are mentors or supporters chosen and prepared for such a potentially demanding role?

Mentors and support

Various models have been developed which describe the progression of beginning teachers towards full competence. Berliner (2001) suggests five stages:

1. novice
2. advanced beginner
3. competent performer
4. proficient
5. expert.

The support provided to novice and beginning teachers is critical to the quality of their immediate professional experiences. It provides an essential foundation if Berliner is correct, although inductees may rarely recognise this at the time, to their longer-term professional learning. Mentoring is one such form of professional support that has received widespread attention in the literature and which has been implemented in a number of pre-service teacher education and induction programmes in various systems during the last two decades. Careful analysis of induction programmes including the new Scottish provision, indicates that certain approaches to mentoring or supporting are not underpinned by appropriate preparation and training of the supporter. This is most notable in relation to areas such as focused reflection and the differences in the supporter role, that is, between the supportive, challenging and assessment roles that are often intertwined and ill-defined. Are mentors prepared for this difficult role and if so what might this involve?

There was an ill-fated attempt to introduce mentoring into Scotland's ITE arrangements (Cameron-Jones and O'Hara, 1997) in the early 1990s which failed because the teacher unions saw this as an imposition by government with inadequate consultation and resourcing and refused to engage with the additional demands on teachers' workload. Post McCrone, times have changed and while still not integrated in ITE, mentoring and coaching are now clearly at the forefront of alternative approaches to CPD in Scotland, especially in relation to developments in leadership preparation and continuing support. There appears to be an 'official' belief or optimism, perhaps unwarranted, that mentoring and coaching are some form of panacea and that the system can instantly capitalise on a range of knowledge, skills, and attributes in teachers and school leaders which have been lying semi-dormant. The new induction scheme promised every new beginner teacher a 'supporter' but the haste with which the scheme was implemented meant that there was little or no preparation or training for these supporter/mentors. This has developed at local level in the past few years but there is little sense as yet of a 'national' approach to mentor development.

Mentors have been generically defined as 'wise and trusted counsellors' suggesting that mentors have protégés that they guide and foster their development. O'Brien and Christie (2005, p. 191) suggest that 'analyses of the mentoring of student and beginning teachers distinguish mentoring from other related types of support'. Mentors are not 'counsellors', not 'buddies' and involvement in the assessment of the beginner teacher for licensing purposes might preclude such personnel from being mentors. Agreed definitions in education of what a mentor is are genuinely difficult to find. What is clear is that there is no template but there are indicators in the literature and practice of what beginner teachers value most in a supporter or mentor (Rippon and Martin, 2003; 2006). Clutterbuck (2001) suggested a range of competences for mentors:

- self-awareness (understanding self);
- communicating;

- sense of proportion / humour;
- interest in developing others;
- goal clarity;
- behavioural awareness (understanding others);
- conceptualising;
- business / professional knowhow;
- committed to own learning;
- relationship management.

Development and enhancement of these competences might usefully form part of a training programme for mentors in induction schemes in education. Interpersonal skills appear to be of paramount importance, some people stress the need for 'emotional intelligence', for example. From the perspective of new teachers and supporters (O'Brien and Christie, 2005), the importance of the interpersonal aspect of a mentoring relationship is evident. It was suggested that trust, calmness, fairness, approachability, honesty, reassurance and a capacity to see things from the probationer's perspective were desirable. One might expect mentors as experienced teachers to be wholly conversant with subject knowledge and teaching and learning methodologies and to be able to discuss these in a coherent and reflective way but there is some evidence noted above that Scottish teachers operating as supporters within the Scheme, in its first year at least, offered few opportunities for such reflective dialogue. Dealing with the tensions inherent in being both a supporter and an assessor in the Scottish approach must be part of a training programme. Supporters need to have experience and knowledge and to possess organisational skills and resourcefulness. They should have the desire to do the job and not be involved only because a new teacher arrives in their department or stage. Training is necessary in observational skills and in giving feedback allied to providing further modelling or resources. A school co-ordinator in our study (O'Brien and Christie, 2005, p. 196) commented tellingly that even with training there will be complexities:

> . . . the same kind of person who might be very positive, very helpful, very easily approachable might be the perfect mentor for very well-motivated students [*sic*] [i.e. probationers] but that same person might be caused a great deal of distress in trying to deal with someone who wasn't performing and maybe somebody scarier might be better.

This is a timely reminder that while specific training is probably best provided most efficiently at educational authority level, school context cannot be ignored and there are strong suggestions that schools were induction is successful have a learning culture, open classrooms, a strong staff development structure (Heilbronn *et al.*, 2002) and a collaborative culture (Williams *et al.*, 2001).

An induction curriculum?

While it is generally accepted that the period of induction is a critical phase in establishing new teachers in the profession, there are wide disparities in the nature of, and the orientation to, teaching, and in degrees of support, mentoring and guidance available. What should be included in an induction programme or curriculum? McNally (2002), has identified three overarching areas of need:

- information and advice for the inevitable difficulties of beginning teaching;
- the nurturing of personal development;
- the maintenance of a critical and reflective approach.

He goes on to outline the development of a set of grounded practical principles for teacher induction, including stability and continuity, collegial support, the availability of key support personnel, a national induction programme with an individualised strand, support for the supporters, and quality assurance.

If we were to outline an induction curriculum what might it look like? Beyond the obvious first day information giving, one could try to construct a list of themes to be addressed such as:

- legal and contractual matters for teachers, a classic human resource management model;
- local policy priorities;
- community information and issues;
- classroom organisation and management including behaviour management;
- theories of teaching and learning, an often under-developed area in teacher conceptualisation;
- current curriculum initiatives and subject-specific knowledge;
- professionalism in teaching and professional development.

There would be myriad sub-themes and issues possible within such a listing. What is missing perhaps is consideration of the individual and his or her needs. How are these identified? How do school managers and leaders meet such needs – is there scope for a personal induction learning plan for new teachers? While this type of broad-brush list is superficially attractive and offers a planning tool, local interpretations of such a list will suggest which might best be met with information and which by professional development. This might include on and off site 'courses'; different forms of experiences within the school, the district and the community; various interactions and reflective experiences with colleagues within and outside the school.

Allied to such a 'curriculum', most increasingly effective induction programmes have recognisable features and include aspects such as:

- orientation;
- reduced timetables;
- mentors with release time;
- opportunities for mentors to be trained and well prepared;
- opportunities to build on prior learning and experience;
- CPD opportunities for all those involved especially beginning teachers;
- access to other forms of support such as websites or CDRoms;
- professional collaboration;
- work-based learning opportunities;
- observation and feedback through professional dialogue;
- recording and portfolio development as 'evidence' of meeting required standards.

Other essential requirements might be:

- better structures to facilitate communication and dialogue;
- the development of collegiality and networks;
- providing a clear distinction between supervisory and developmental aspects of the school's role;
- and better partnerships between teacher education institutions and schools.

Managing induction

Too often, induction has been a neglected area characterised by a brief introduction of the new teacher(s) to the school. Depending on the number of new starters, sometimes a conference is held, where new colleagues are presented with a school handbook, a list of important people, emergency numbers – if they are lucky – and issued with a brain-numbing timetable and an expectation that the new recruit will prove up to the task. At the district level they will be invited to another conference and be given similar information. However, this new teacher is expected to come to terms with and absorb a set of well-established rules, relationships and pecking orders, ways of behaving especially in relation to staffroom seating arrangements according to anecdotes, and the unspoken understandings that give a particular school its unique character. Beginning teaching resembles a process of transition or a rite of passage.

There is a need for overall management of induction. At the wider school level it is important to monitor standards, to ensure consistency within the school and conduct appropriate external liaison not just in relation to potential 'failing' probationers. It is the school, of course, which is the immediate community of practice for the new teacher. So where there is an ideal, supportive collegial environment, the key role of the headteacher is to build on it; otherwise the headteacher should assist in developing it.

Creating a context for induction and early professional development is a key task of the headteacher. Two key terms that pervade the literature about teacher development and learning are 'communities' and 'culture'. Chris Day (1999, p. 78) defines 'culture' as being about

> people in the organisational setting, characterised by the ways in which values, beliefs, prejudices and behaviour are played out within the micro-political processes of school life.

Tickle (2000a; 2000b) argues for communities of reflective practitioners in order that teacher development might become more than private introspection. Our research (Christie *et al.*, 2003) indicated that in our case study schools, despite the emphasis in recent times on substantial professional development, there was sketchy evidence of a 'learning community' and enhanced professional culture. One of the roles for headteachers in most systems, and a key role at that, is the assessment of the probationer. Often, particularly in secondary schools, this is a delegated responsibility in practice, but this implies that principals or headteachers and other school staff, particularly mentors, have a clear understanding of what makes a good teacher that is shared by the probationer. The existence of a standard can often help, our own research suggests strongly that assessors in schools still do not use the SfR and remain unfamiliar with it and continue to rely on a series of traditional indicators of competence or 'gut feelings'. This may deny appropriate entitlement to support and development. The Scottish experience is mirrored in England where NQTs are acutely aware of variability in interpretations for assessment against the Induction Standards by different experienced staff. There are differences of provision across schools and NQTs are concerned that induction should be equitably implemented. Satisfactory performance during the induction period is a condition of full registration, thus the role of the headteacher and staff has important formal characteristics in addition to the impact induction has on future teachers' perceptions of the nature and quality of professional life.

Direct engagement with and management of the entire process by the headteacher is necessary. All staff need to be made aware of the school's induction provision and offered opportunities to contribute to NQTs' programmes of support and training.

Another often neglected responsibility is monitoring and evaluation. How do you know what is going on about induction in your school and what evidence can you produce? In the formal evaluation of the new system in England (Totterdell *et al.*, 2002), many NQTs said that certain entitlements were not consistently being provided by their schools. They made strong calls for their schools' induction provision to be monitored by educational authorities much more tightly than at present. Christie *et al.* (2003) indicate that there was little evidence of appreciation that monitoring and evaluation of what the school was doing with respect to induction was important. Perhaps at that early stage the emphasis was on structures, familiarisation with the new processes and getting the induction scheme off to a good start. Or is this evidence of complacency and lack of depth of analysis even with a culture in Scotland of self-evaluation based on *How Good is Our School*? (SOEID, 1996). The continuing monitoring and evaluation of the induction process; the role, understanding of and use of the Standard; the preparation and ongoing development of mentors are all critical management tasks as is the communication of developments or concerns to educational authorities and other stakeholders such as GTCS. If induction for beginning teachers is to be the foundation of CPD for all new teachers and a gate-keeping process for the profession, the new approaches cannot be allowed to become moribund as the probation arrangements had become.

Chapter 5

INDUCTION FOR EXPERIENCED TEACHERS

Much work on induction in business and managerial settings has focused on those who change jobs either within or between organisations. In teaching, in contrast, 'induction' has usually been reserved for those entering the profession, with apparently little consideration of the induction needs of more experienced teachers, even in circumstances where it might be identified that these needs were substantial, for example where acting heads take over their role at short notice.

Induction for more experienced teachers represents therefore a fairly clean sheet. Although there has been both in-post and preparatory training for entry into some promoted posts, this does not address all induction needs by any means. The issues spelt out in Chapter 1 about beginning a new post at any stage are core to this discussion, in relation to social integration (and scope to develop micropolitical and/or organisational literacy), understanding of systems and identifying and beginning to meet new professional development needs.

It is important for this discussion also to recognise that there is variety in the kinds of career moves teachers make. While some seek vertical progression (promotion) others seek more horizontal routes, transferring to similar posts at the same level in the same or a different school or changing sector / phase. Although many systems, of which Scotland is one, have both a career ladder of posts and a framework of hierarchical standards for CPD, it is clear from the evidence (Draper *et al.*, 1998b; Draper and Sharp, 2006; James and Whiting, 1998) that many teachers do not wish to climb the ladder to headship. Some choose never to seek promotion while others happily and deliberately stop at various steps on the ladder. It is important to note therefore that most of the limited evidence on induction after the early stages of teachers' careers relates to induction into senior posts and particularly to headship. Information on transfers (voluntary or involuntary) between schools or shifts between sectors is very sparse.

Job change during a teaching career

There are several dimensions to changes in post after the induction period: moving posts within school, an internal shift, and moving between schools and also possibly employing authorities, an external shift. External shifts may be of several kinds, moving to another school in the same local authority or to another authority, and may be accompanied by other changes: changing locality, professional networks, domestic moves, a change in social networks, a change in commuting distance. These are captured in Figure 4 (opposite).

There may be a transfer to a similar post, or a differently focused post at the same level in the job hierarchy, both horizontal shifts. Or the move may involve a vertical shift to a different level of post: a promotion or a demotion. In addition, some moves may be temporary and others permanent, and each will have its own features and implications for induction.

The limited evidence on induction beyond the beginning teacher stage on the whole suggests that there is much that could be done to improve induction into posts beyond the early years of a teaching career, in that the need for new learning appears to go either unrecognised or unprovided for and scope is missed for contribution. It is this area in particular that reveals the low level of systematic human resource support available to school staff. Given the role of induction in supporting commitment as well as development, a failure to address needs when new posts with their new demands are taken up means an opportunity is lost to cement involvement in working in teaching. Industrial and commercial organisations increasingly recognise that when staff change jobs they are more effective more quickly if given the information and support they need to ease into the new role. There is surely no reason why this should be different in teaching? The point when a new member of staff becomes detached from their previous work is a vulnerable stage when there is a clear risk to commitment. Supporting the development of commitment in the new post seems essential if retention in teaching is to be sustained and effectiveness in the new post to be enabled.

Of course, it is inevitable that some will leave the profession, for a range of reasons. Some may wish to move to other work, some may seek other lives. Significant loss of experienced teachers, however, becomes a matter of concern on two grounds. The loss of experience to the overall staff team and its impact on the support available to less experienced teachers is one. A problem also arises when the pool of prospective senior staff becomes too small and questions are raised, as they have been (Williams, 2003; Walker *et al.*, 2003) about the quantity and/or quality of applicants for senior posts including headship. Where there are teacher supply problems the pool is likely to be smaller; where teachers are demoralised (perhaps through a lack of early success) or ill managed they may believe this is not a job for them. If many desist then headship becomes a matter of recruitment rather than selection from a group of candidates, and school leaders are chosen by themselves, by those who come forward rather than selected by others. With an ageing profession and many staff approaching retirement (and 'winding

Figure 4: Dimensions of transition in job change: the basis of a plan for induction

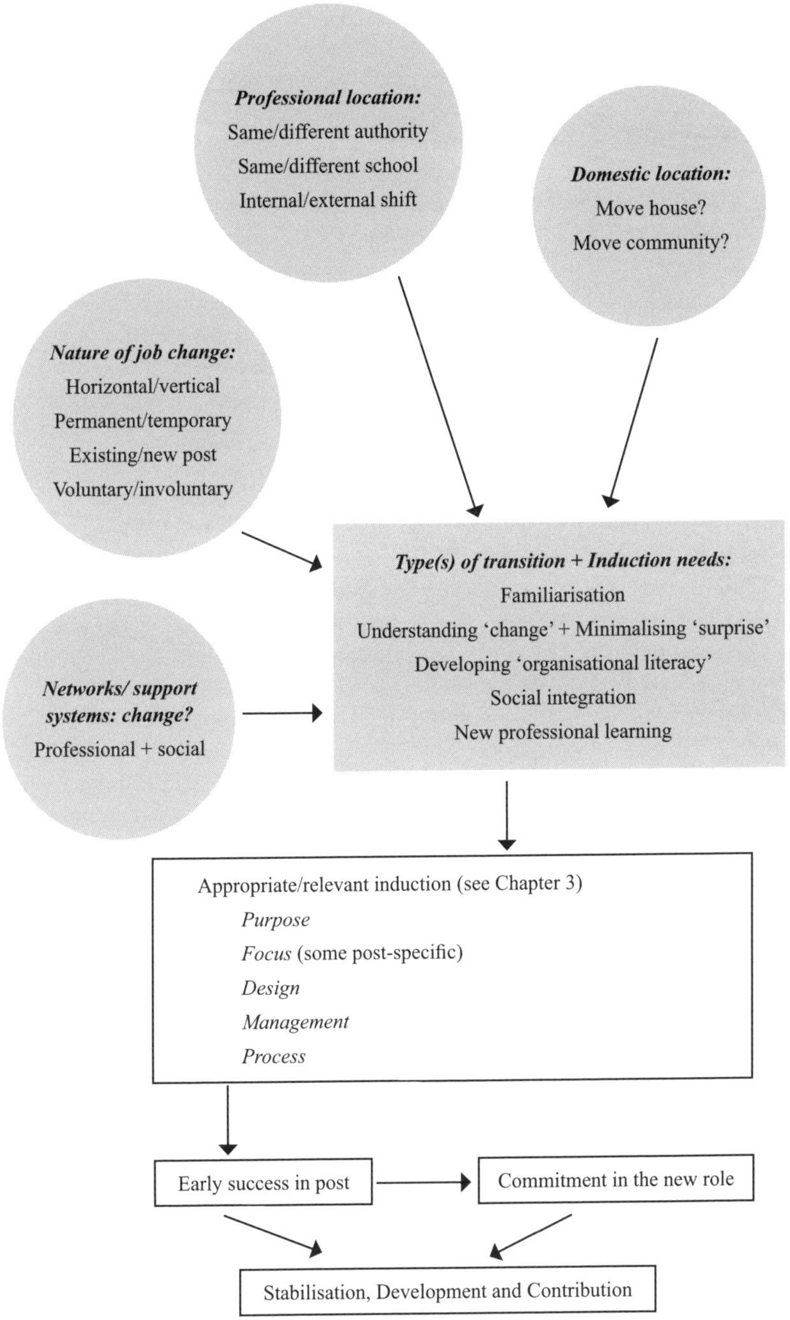

down'), the loss of more experienced teachers is a matter of considerable potential concern. A recent study (Sharp and Draper, 2000) suggested that teachers left at all stages of their careers, not only in the early years and at retirement.

The transition of moving post is a time of disconnection and reconnection. If induction is inadequate and there is a failure to cement the commitment of those in transition in teaching then retention problems are more likely to follow. While there has been an acknowledgement of the importance of encouraging retention in the early years of a teaching career, less attention has been paid to later stages. This may in part be due to the complexity of the task. It may well appear simpler to provide induction for those at similar career stages, like beginning teachers, although this is to underplay the variations in work and other experience which should shape their induction. For more experienced teachers moving to different posts in differing circumstances the task of developing appropriate induction is greater but there is no less need for it to be done!

Some findings on induction for more experienced teachers

In a study of new primary heads, Draper and McMichael (1998b) found heads reported many surprises. They had expected to feel autonomous, in charge of their school, able to take forward their ideas and to support the school's development through monitoring of teaching and learning. Instead they found their time taken up with making sense of the school's administrative systems, with little time for observing in classrooms. They found themselves in a role defined by managerialism and bureaucracy but with little scope for leading or for enhancing effectiveness. They were surprised by how much respect their role attracted and how they had to tailor their comments more than before since even 'throw away' lines were taken more seriously than before. The workload was even higher than expected and they reported little support from the employing authority once appointed. Human resource support for transition was limited. The CPD needs of new heads as developing managers were apparently invisible. While the formal qualification for headship brought a new training structure focused on interpersonal and other management skills, the greatest problems they found were in understanding and managing administrative systems. Absence of good human resource support for new heads left them vulnerable, less effective and less likely to have the early success which is important for commitment, and undermined their confidence about being able to do the job of headteacher. A partial solution would be to improve induction at school and local authority levels, but the study also raises questions about the design of the headteacher's role.

A parallel study of new secondary heads (Draper and McMichael, 2000a) again suggested that understanding the context was key to making progress in the new role, and that this was influenced by the extent to which the senior management team they had joined was co-operative and helped to initiate them into schools, and also by the support offered by other headteachers. Local authority support was limited, especially after appointment. There was evidence of the significant amount of change between one school and another that reinforces the need for induction. As a start, a period for handover might alleviate some of the difficulties encountered.

A third study of temporary acting headteachers (Draper and McMichael, 2003a) brought several dimensions of induction into sharp focus. Appointments were often made at very short notice, even when the appointment itself was not a response to a crisis. There was therefore little preparation for the role and little clarity about likely length of contract. The absence of formal appointment procedures (more normal was the nomination of a member of staff in the school, though some were external appointments) meant the opportunity to ask questions and achieve clarity about the role was lost. There was little or no handover or induction, yet the temporary head was generally expected to both keep the school running and to take it forward.

Understanding differences in role were not, however, confined to vertical moves. A study of teachers converting from secondary to primary teaching (Draper, 1997) found that there was much new learning to be done about both context and the role.

So what is required? Making induction work

Drawing upon the issues raised in Chapter 3, this section will focus on the purposes, focus, design, management and process of induction.

The purposes of induction

The general *purpose* of induction, to support new arrivals, should be clear by now but there will be specifics which need to be identified for each new arrival. What needs to be considered in planning for induction for experienced teachers moving post?

New experienced staff need opportunities to integrate socially and professionally, to learn the ropes and key policies, priorities and procedures for their new role. Given that it is clear that different schools have different systems, newly arrived experienced staff will have much to unlearn as well as to learn, although it is important that it is possible for useful or interesting practice from previous schools to be harnessed rather than set aside. Even those who move internally may find there is much to learn, for different roles have different foci and different sub groupings of staff adopt different approaches.

Each type of move will create its own requirements, including the focus, need for new information, need to negotiate a role, need for professional development opportunities. For even internal shifts of role require support in order that people can settle into posts quickly and others can acknowledge and work with them in their new role. This chapter will draw upon the Nicholson and West (1988) model of preparation, encounter, adjustment and stabilisation (which was discussed in Chapter 1) to structure reflections on these varying circumstances. Louis (1980) draws attention to the need to distinguish change (inevitable differences between posts) and surprise (discrepancies between expectations and the reality of experience). While change may be a deliberate motivator in a decision to move job, 'surprise' may cause difficulties in settling in especially if the surprises are negative, that is, the new experience being less good or more complicated than expected. It is argued that what is needed is an attempt to ensure that job/career decision making is as realistically informed as possible, by a good understanding of likely change and the minimisation of surprise. In addition it is argued that the provision of *information* is insufficient in part because, as with beginning teachers, it is the provision of *support* that enables new incumbents to identify scope for, and to make, their own contribution and development.

In addition to the other purposes explored earlier, induction may also be viewed as part of succession management. There are two important points here. Induction offers a way of enabling achievement, giving staff new to roles a positive early experience on which to build their learning. It also provides an opportunity to review roles and consider whether they are manageable.

Fink (2005) draws attention to the importance of succession management pointing out that with high leadership turnover, leadership succession is very important, and that in turn this generates two types of need. One is the need to support development and the other is a need for support to enable achievement, especially early achievement, in order to retain staff.

A NAPA study (1997) suggests succession management is 'a deliberate and systemic effort to project leadership requirements, identify a pool of high potential candidates, develop leadership competencies in those candidates, through intentional learning experiences, and then select from among a pool of leaders', all of which implies careful human resource practice to identify and *develop* staff. The identification process is unlikely to be easy since there is no clear agreement on the characteristics of good leaders, and in a rapidly changing context it is reasonable to expect that future leaders should not simply be replacements/clones of current leaders, although Fink (2005) argues that the public sector remains more likely than the private sector to favour clones of previous leaders. It seems likely that in a rapidly changing context it may be more important to have a capacity to learn. Having identified a group of potential leaders, there is then an opportunity to prepare them for a new post. A proactive approach to ensuring there is such a pool has been identified as essential in some systems (for example, Williams, 2003; Gronn and Rawlings-Sanaei, 2003; Draper and McMichael, 2003b) given past experience of crisis, but such a clearly developmental strategy remains unusual in the public sector, according to Fink.

In order to support as smooth a transition as possible into a new post an induction system should clarify the nature of roles and the demands and expectations which lie with them. Induction itself thus also offers an opportunity to review the role. If this process reveals that expectations are unrealistic, that only superman or superwoman will be able to do the job, then this raises the question of whether the role needs to be redesigned! The fact that a large number of deputy heads, for example, did not wish to seek headship because of the nature of the role (with which they were quite familiar) (Draper and McMichael, 1998a) suggests that seeing induction as supporting new staff to fit their new role is a limited view. Planning induction may also identify inconsistencies and anomalies related to a role which require action to address them.

Focus of induction

While the focus may vary with role, there seem to be some commonalities of need. Clearly there are many dimensions of variation between schools including nature of catchment areas, academic results, relative focus on sport, art and academic work which are at least partly accessible to research prior to application. However, new arrivals in promoted posts in unfamiliar schools report few opportunities to find out about many aspects of the role and setting. The research which exists highlights significant differences between schools in their administrative systems and procedures as well as culture, climate and nature of the pupil and parent body.

Along with identifying differences between the old and the new job, there is a need to become familiar with the school as an organisation to become, in Kuzmic's term, organisationally literate: becoming familiar with the actual (as opposed to the notional) workings of the organisation, including its informal organisation and underpinning power structures, history, priorities and agendas. This involves many of the features which were identified as part of initial induction, including coming to know the people, the key policies, the key priorities (for example those highlighted in the current school development plan), the physical layout of the school, who to go to for what information etc., how to access professional development opportunities: aspects which would go under a general heading of familiarisation with the school and how it operates. It is all too easy to underestimate how differently schools work. Also needed is an understanding of how organisations vary from their formal structure and public presentation . . . less easy to uncover but just as, if not more, real. The internal workings of institutions shape the organisation at least as much as do the formal structures but are often very difficult to access in a systematic sustained way. Furthermore, this kind of information may sometimes be presented in a partisan and individual way. In addition, the potential applicant may be offered much more formal information on how the organisation is supposed to work than how it actually works in practice.

Design

In design terms, the scale of other changes with which new arrivals will be dealing will be varied. Some may have moved school and colleagues as well as house and community, other may not have done so. Some may have moved authority, others not.

All these differences, as portrayed in Figure 4 above, suggest that, to at least an extent, induction must be tailored to the person and their needs for information and support.

It is perhaps worth remembering that many staff developing induction programmes may well themselves have had no effective induction and the process may therefore be one of trial and error. Some of the information and understanding that is needed, especially of the formal and public variety can be (and is quite often) disseminated to new staff in the form of a staff handbook and associated material which is given to a new member of staff during the preparation period before a post is taken up. However the relevance of some of this material may be in doubt. Information offered, which reflects the understandings of those already integrated into the organisation, may not be the information needed or prioritised by new entrants. In addition, there may or may not be much time for the new arrival to absorb this material. Those finishing work in one school may be concerned with 'tidying up' the old job to leave things in such a way that a new incumbent can take over as easily as possible. Visits to the new school, where relevant and feasible, are an opportunity to re-orient as well as to meet some of the people and form part of the *preparation* stage.

Some information about the school will have been made available during any selection procedure. However, some moves arise without selection, for example, through compulsory transfer of staff between schools or for temporary acting posts. As noted above, acting headships often came about by nomination: appointment without selection. Recruitment and selection where they happen are important elements of preparation. They shape the new member of staff's expectations and attitudes about the school and/or the role. The absence of these processes reduces the opportunity for staff to ask questions about the new role and expectations as well as making them vulnerable to questions about their suitability which has not been tested 'in the market place'.

Further elements of the design of induction will relate to what and who new staff need to know and by when: the post may be a useful guide in deciding which matters are of highest priority and which may wait and identifying likely areas of rapid learning need and providing for these. However, design must also allow for the new arrival to shape their engagement and to identify ways of making a contribution, drawing on their previous experience rather than just fitting into a space.

Induction essentially begins with the advertisement for a post. Subsequent recruitment and selection processes are important times for achieving a realistic preview of the new role. The availability of useful information and contacts for questions are important elements of the preparation period. Those moving roles within a school, whether horizontally or vertically, may well find that it is assumed they have little need for induction since they 'know the school'. However, what they need to know for their new post may be different from what they know from their previous post.

Management

Schools are complex organisations and many people will share responsibility for the induction of new staff, irrespective of their experience. The management and monitoring of induction will thus be important to ensure that key needs are covered. As with beginning teachers, mentors, given time and training to support new staff and who are familiar with the new role being taken up, are likely to be useful. As with any teacher development, time available will be limited so duplication needs to be avoided and key needs must be identified to ensure they are met as much as possible. A period of handover where existing, departing and new staff work alongside each other is a common feature of staff changes in many organisations. In schools it appears to be much less common and much institutional and role understanding may thus be lost in the transition.

For new heads in particular there may be no obvious person to guide them through the systems. Their very centrality in inducting others means their own needs may be overlooked. There is a clear case for the distribution of tasks between school, local authority and headteacher colleagues, but without careful planning the enterprise may fail to be effective. Mercer's (1996) work highlighting the isolation of the headteacher role reinforces this concern. Fink (2005) suggests that the new head needs to take up a peripheral position in the early period in post in order to integrate into the professional learning community prior to initiating change. Findings from new heads suggest there is often little scope for such peripheral engagement.

Process

Once new staff arrive in any level of post they need support and permission 'not to know' how things work. This caused particular problems for headteachers (Draper and McMichael, 1998b). Existing staff moving roles within a school may need time and opportunity to renegotiate their working relationships with existing colleagues. Schools in particular have an extended period before some events 'come round again' so in Nicholson and West's terms the 'encounter' stage may overlap with the 'adjustment' phase and it may be some time before new staff can feel they are fully aware of what is required. It may be even longer before they are confident they can do what is expected. There must also be space for them to reshape roles, to take them forward, to develop themselves and to make their own contribution to the role and school. The commitment to CPD as an entitlement for all makes this more possible, provided individual professional development needs are acknowledged and the learning needs of new staff are distinguished from the development needs of those who are already established in post.

The model for beginning teachers (Chapter 1 and Chapter 3) highlighted the dimensions of direction and support, and suggested four modes of induction: facilitative, directive coaching, neglecting top-down and laissez-faire. From the evidence that exists it would be fair to conclude that many teachers moving into new posts experience *laissez-faire* induction at best. In more prescriptive managerialist contexts their experience may, however, match *neglecting top-down* induction, even though for many career moves there is not a set standard to be met. However, this may have contrasting consequences. It may lead to a lack of appreciation of the amount of new learning required and therefore an absence of support for such learning. There may be, as in the old days of probation, a lack of clarity about what is wanted or needed in the post leaving the new arrival unsure about how well they are doing. There may be an assumption they will do the job as the previous incumbent did. Some new heads felt 'haunted' by expectations deriving from their predecessor's style of working (Draper and McMichael, 1998b) and found they had to make substantial efforts to develop their own style. Above all, however, for induction to be effective the process should be both developmental and supportive.

For schools to move forward, social integration and acculturation will not be enough: there needs to be scope and support for development and for contributions to be made to policy and practice.

Chapter 6

THE FUTURE OF INDUCTION

In the preceding five chapters we have explored the nature of induction and its place in the support of staff in new posts. Chapter 1 defined the nature and significance of induction and offered a model for differentiating different forms and outcomes of the induction process. In Chapter 2 the changing context and structure of teachers' work and the changing and increasingly central role of professional development both highlighted the need for induction being regarded as a key opportunity for building commitment to a new role and to CPD within that role. The great variety in forms of induction explored in Chapter 3 suggests that contexts shape the development of induction as a support mechanism, and suggests that thought must be given to the purposes, focus, management, design and process of induction. Jones and Alexiadou's claim that 'travelling policies' are shaped by 'embedded practices' seems particularly relevant to this chapter and to Chapter 4 which explores the structures, standards and mechanisms of induction and teacher development. The bulk of the evidence in Chapters 3 and 4 is drawn from the induction of beginning teachers. Chapter 5 clarifies that many of the same issues arise for those new to posts throughout a career in teaching and makes a plea for more careful consideration of the needs of experienced teachers moving through a transition into a new role and serves as a reminder that headship is not the goal of all. This final chapter draws together a series of issues that have emerged earlier in the course of our discussion and we will make suggestions for the future of induction for all teachers taking up a new post.

The future of induction

As induction becomes more developed there are a number of potential pitfalls that are evident:

- Induction is multi-faceted and there is a danger that some aspects may be developed at the expense of others. For example, a very strong focus on professional development is laudable but could mean, as has been seen in current evidence available especially for more experienced teachers in schools, that learning about the 'nuts and bolts' of a post and its context are overlooked. Nicholson and West's model is helpful here. They highlight that while preparation may give clear indications, experience in the early stages ('encounter' and 'adjustment') is necessary to construct a fuller understanding of the post and its setting. They suggest that reaching the stage of stabilisation indicates a readiness to pick up new developmental opportunities beyond those which assist in 'settling in'. To attempt to move forward before the basis systems are understood to a degree which enables day-to-day functioning may be unhelpful. Of course there are also dangers in being too acclimatised, for there is a need also for new staff to contribute to the development of the school. Fresh eyes and ideas are a valuable resource for organisational development, if the organisation is open to suggestion. Sustaining a concept of induction as a collaborative process is necessary for new arrivals to feel their questions and suggestions are welcome. A conception of induction as 'telling new staff how it is' will mean that possibilities for review and refreshment are lost.

- Planning for induction also gives an opportunity to review a post and expectations of what that post should incorporate. The potential for redrawing responsibilities and expectations is live whenever a post is to be filled. The design of induction round specific posts offers a time for considering whether the role is manageable for a real rather than a superperson! Part of the public sector ethos may indeed be to be idealistic and aspirational, however if new staff are faced with impossible jobs this tends to be demoralising rather than stimulating. In addition, if staff get used to the idea of 'doing what you can' of an impossible job, then there has to be concern about whether what are done are the tasks of highest priority. Feldman and Brett's notion of a 'realistic preview' of a post has implications for all those involved: it should enable the aspiring post holder to be clear what is expected and required . . . and there is an onus on those designing the job to ensure it is doable. People can do no more than they can do . . . expecting the impossible is, in the end, irresponsible and threatens retention. Concern registered over the supply of school principals is a clear example. If the design of senior posts in schools is such that many do not wish to apply for them, then this should be a matter of continuing concern until it is resolved. If this is the case for other posts in schools then the same applies.

- Planning and reviewing are not enough: resources and monitoring are needed too.

  The history of induction for beginning teachers is full of examples of unrealised good intention to support new teachers. For induction to work effectively for all, the plans made have to be implemented. This means that plans must be both realistic and resourced: if they are inadequate in either respect then it will not work as well as it should and that is a cost the system and its learners will continue to carry.

- A careful consideration of the role and implementation of standards is needed. They may operate as guides or straitjackets for the development of new staff. Narrow definitions of teaching and of key elements of teachers' work are of little benefit to complex high skills professional performance. Standards are useful in so far as they capture key elements of work, but they need not be prescriptive in themselves. Neither should they be purely aspirational but again like post previews, they should be feasible, which seems more likely if their development emanates from a collaborative and genuinely consultative process, where their content is attested to by those who currently work in the relevant roles. Commonly, it seems that the prescriptive aspect comes when standards are implemented in practice and particularly in relation to assessment, monitoring and evaluation when the good intentions of the standards may be lost in a haze of accountability.

  The introduction of standards has had a significant impact on the provision and resourcing of induction for new teachers and this is to be welcomed. The question is whether the resourcing of induction, as an investment, can be acknowledged as valuable in itself without an associated need to be fully prescriptive about its outcomes, thus enabling more facilitative induction processes to be developed. There is also a need to regularly review standards to prevent the system which circumscribes professional development from becoming ossified.

- The style of induction is thus important: the relative focus on proof and development, for example, shapes whether the key experience is one of support and innovation or evaluation and accountability. A focus on development creates obligations on those who support and those who are supported. This raises again the issue of the desired outcome of induction: a self-evaluating and self-critical professional who can identify and pursue their own professional needs . . . or an accommodating implementer of policy?

If the new member of staff is to make a contribution, to do more than just fit in, then the style must allow for, even enable, questioning and the suggestion of new ideas, ways of doing and ways of thinking. If the inductee plays merely a passive role in the process then the potential for change which new staff, at all career stages, bring with them will be lost. Consequently, the inductee should be actively and collaboratively engaged in the process of induction.

- Underpinning much of the thinking about induction is the expectation of a system which invests in human resource management and support for teachers. This is not a quest for paternalistic direction but a plea for a level of support appropriate to busy and forward-looking professionals, for the facilitation of independence and for capacity building. The experiences of acting heads are a clear example where a legitimate expectation of support was not met. Conventionally appointed new heads also felt abandoned after appointment. These are symptoms of a system that does not recognise the reasonable expectations of new appointees. If new staff are to settle in and to grow and learn in a new post they will need useful support.

  The contractual arrangements associated with a new post need consideration in this regard. Where work is casualised and / or temporary, as in the case of some beginning teachers and acting heads, particular attention needs to be paid to the need for preparation, key information being available and a recognition that support and provision of and resourcing for professional development may be, at best, patchy.

- Teachers have significant skills, indeed they have transferable skills which are highly marketable in an increasingly high skills work context. They represent significant social capital, for example, in organising and planning, and in interpersonal skills. These skills are much sought after in the new world of work and the high skills workforce. We therefore ignore alternative work opportunities for teachers at our peril. As work and career patterns change, some enter teaching early and leave early, while others enter after work experience elsewhere which shapes their expectations.

- Professional training, recruitment and induction of teachers are resource intensive and therefore expensive. The concept of payback period, that is, how long a teacher has to teach for this investment to be recouped, is valuable in recognising how important it is to retain teachers. The calculation of payback is further complicated in several ways, by continuing investment in professional development, by the cost of lost experience to schools when skilled and experienced staff leave, the cost of renewed recruitment and induction and the cost of disrupted education for pupils. The benefits of induction, settling in quickly, a positive focus on CPD, the development of commitment and a reduced risk of leaving can all be part of the equation if induction is taken seriously. In the face of all this investment, the costs of induction are relatively small yet they offer significant rewards.

Ideally, therefore, the future of induction will be that it is developed for all new arrivals in posts in schools, teachers ***and others****, and that the process of settling in to what are very different establishments will be eased. New staff will then be able to move forward more quickly into fuller engagement with their role and its and their further development.*

Transition into a new work role makes many demands on both new incumbents and those who support them. Induction is here argued to have many dimensions, including the need to understand the new context, its policies and expectations, its ways of working, its sources of support and resources; the need to integrate into the staff group in order to access these resources and support and key information required; the need to facilitate learning for and in the new role; the need for support and early success to enable the development of confidence in the new role; the need to identify opportunities to make a contribution of one's own. These are substantial demands to make on many staff in a school – teaching and support staff, promoted and unpromoted colleagues – and they signal that induction is a lengthy process, not something that can be completed in the first few days of taking up a new post. However, as Bubb and Earley (2006, p. 211) comment: 'There are two sets of learners within schools: young people and adults: We neglect either at our peril.' Good induction does not come cheap but it represents an investment in new staff, and, like education ('If you think education is expensive try ignorance'), the costs of failure to induct lie in wasted potential, lower commitment, higher staff turnover, less learning and disrupted education.

REFERENCES

Acker, S. (1999) *The Reality of Teachers' Work*, London: Cassell

Ackroyd, S., Ball, S. Thomson, P. and Tolbert, P. (2005) *The Oxford Handbook of Work and Organisation*, Oxford: Oxford University Press

Alexandrou, A., Field, K. and Mitchell, H. (2005) 'Emerging themes', in Alexandrou, A. Field, K. and Mitchell, H. (eds) (2005) *The Continuing Professional Development of Educators: Emerging European Issues*, Oxford: Symposium Books, pp. 139–46

American Federation of Teachers (2001) *Beginning Teacher Induction: The Essential Bridge*, Educational Issues Policy Brief 13, Washington, DC: AFT

Angus Council (2002) *Teacher Induction Scheme – Guidelines for* Schools, Angus: Education Department

Asia-Pacific Economic Co-operation ministerial group (APEC) (1997) From Students of Teaching to Teachers of Students: Teacher Induction Around the Pacific Rim (online). Available from URL: www.ed.gov/pubs/APEC (accessed 28 April 2006)

Atkinson, J. (1984) 'Manpower strategies for flexible organisations', *Personnel Management*, Vol. 16, No. 8, pp. 28–31

Australian Council for Educational Research (2004) *Evaluation of the Standards and Professional Learning Project 2003*, report to the Standards and Professional Learning Branch, Victorian Institute of Teaching. ACER: Teaching and Learning Research Program

Ball, S. J. (1994) *The Micropolitics of the School: Towards a Theory of School Organisation*, London: Methuen

Ball, S. J. (2003) 'Teachers' souls and the terrors of performativity', *Journal of Education Policy*, Vol. 18, No. 2, pp. 215–28

Banks, F. and Mayes, A. S. (eds) (2001) *Early Professional Development for Teachers*, London: David Fulton

Barrington, R. (2000) 'An investigation into the induction period which considers the perspectives of NQTs and their induction tutors', paper presented at the British Educational Research Association annual conference, Cardiff, September

Barton, L. and Walker, S. (1981) *Schools, Teachers and Teaching*, Lewes: Falmer

Berliner, D. (2001) 'Teacher expertise', in Banks and Mayes (eds) (2001), pp. 20–26

Beyer, L. E. (2002) 'The politics of standardization: teacher education in the USA', *Journal of Education for Teaching*, Vol. 28, No. 3, pp. 239–45

Bolam, R. (1986) 'Conceptually in-service', in Hopkins, D. (ed.) (1986) *In-Service Training and Educational Development*, London: Croom-Helm

Brock, P. (2002) 'Towards establishing and implementing a standards framework in NSW Quality Teaching Awards process: a personal perspective', *Unicorn*, Vol. 28, No. 1, pp. 10–15

Bryce, T. G. K. and Humes, W. (eds) (2003) *Scottish Education, Second Edition, Post-Devolution*, Edinburgh: Edinburgh University Press

Bubb, S. and Earley, P. (2006) 'Induction rites and wrongs', *Journal of In-Service Education*, Vol. 32, No. 1, pp. 5–12

Bubb, S., Earley, P. and Totterdell, M. (2005) 'Accountability and responsibility: "rogue" school leaders and the induction of new teachers in England', *Oxford Review of Education*, Vol. 31, No. 2, pp. 255–72

Bubb, S., Heilbronn, R., Jones, C., Totterdell, M. and Bailey, M. (2002) *Improving Induction: Research Based Best Practice for Schools*, London: RoutledgeFalmer

Bullough, R. (1997) *First-Year Teacher: A Case Study*, New York: Teachers College Press

Burbank, M. D. and Kauchak, D. (2003) 'An alternative model for professional development: investigations into professional collaboration', *Teaching and Teacher Education*, Vol. 19, No. 5, pp. 499–514

Burns, R. B. (1982) *Self-Concept Development and Education*, Eastbourne : Holt, Rinehart and Winston

Cameron-Jones, M. and O'Hara, P. (1997) 'Support and challenge in teacher education', *British Educational Research Journal*, Vol. 23, No. 1, pp. 15–25

Casey, C. (1995) *Work, Self and Society*, London: Routledge

Chambers English Dictionary (1990) Edinburgh: Chambers

Chartered Institute of Personnel and Development (CIPD) (2006) Managing the Psychological Contract (online). Available at URL: www.cipd.co.uk/subjects/empreltns/psycntrct/psycontr.htm (accessed 31 May 2006)

Christie, F., Draper, J. and O'Brien, J. (2003) *A Study of the Induction Scheme for Beginning Secondary Teachers in Scotland*, Edinburgh: University of Edinburgh, Centre for Educational Leadership

Christie, F. and O'Brien, J. (2005) 'A continuing professional development framework for Scottish teachers: steps, stages, continuity or connections?' in Alexandrou, A., Field, K. and Mitchell, H. (eds) (2005) *The Continuing Professional Development of Educators: Emerging European Issues*, Oxford: Symposium Books, pp. 93–110

Chubbuck, S. M., Clift, R. T., Allard, J. and Quinlan, J. (2001) 'Playing it safe as a novice teacher: implications for programs for new teachers', *Journal of Teacher Education*, Vol. 52, No. 5, pp. 365–76

Clutterbuck, D. (2001) *Everyone Needs a Mentor*, London: Chartered Institute of Personnel and Development

Conlon, T. (2004) 'A failure of delivery: the United Kingdom's New Opportunities Fund programme of teacher training in information and computer technology', *Journal of In-Service Education*, Vol. 30, No. 1, pp. 115–39

Connell, R. W. (1985) *Teachers' Work*, Hemel Hempstead: Allen and Unwin

Darling-Hammond, L. (1990) 'Teachers and teaching: signs of a changing profession', in Houston, W. R. (ed.) *Handbook of Research on Teacher Education*, New York: Macmillan, pp. 267–90

Day, C. (1999) *Developing Teacher: The Challenge of Lifelong Learning*, London: Falmer

Day C. (2004) 'Understanding variations in the work and lives of teachers: interim findings of a four year national multi-site research project', paper presented at the annual meeting of the American Educational Research Association, San Diego, California, April

Department for Education and Employment (1999) *The Induction Period for Newly Qualified Teachers*, Circular 5/99, London: DfEE

Department for Education and Skills (2000) *The National Standards for Headteachers*, London: DfES

Draper, J. (1997) 'Converting from secondary to primary: strategic or magnetic reasons?' *School Leadership and Management*, Vol. 17, No. 3, pp. 343–56

Draper, J., Fraser, H., Raab, A. and Taylor, W. (1998a) *Probationers on Supply*, Edinburgh: Edinburgh University

Draper, J., Fraser, H., Sharp, S., Raab, A. and Taylor, W. (1997) *Routes into Primary Teaching*, research report for Scottish Office Education and Industry Department and the General Teaching Council, Edinburgh: Moray House Institute

Draper, J., Fraser, H., Smith, D. and Taylor, W. (1991) *A Study of Probationers*, Edinburgh: Moray House Institute

Draper, J., Fraser, H. and Taylor, W. (1997) 'Teachers at work: early experiences of professional development', *British Journal of In-Service Education*, Vol. 23, No. 2, pp. 283–95

Draper, J., Fraser, H. and Taylor, W. (1998b) 'Teachers' careers: accident or design?' *Teacher Development*, Vol. 2, No. 3, pp. 373–84

Draper, J. and Forrester, V. (2004) *Teacher development in the 21st century: contested and contrasted*, paper given at SERA conference, Perth, November

Draper, J. and McMichael, P. (1998a) 'Preparing a profile: likely applicants for primary headship', *Educational Management Administration*, Vol. 26, No. 2, pp. 161–72

Draper, J. and McMichael, P. (1998b) 'Making sense of primary headship', *School Leadership and Management*, Vol. 18, No. 2, pp. 197–211

Draper, J. and McMichael, P. (2000a) 'Contextualising new headship', *School Leadership and Management*, Vol. 20, No. 4, pp. 459–73

Draper, J. and McMichael, P. (2000b) 'Secondary school identities and career decision making', *Scottish Educational Review*, Vol. 32, No. 2, pp. 155–67

Draper, J. and McMichael, P. (2003a) 'Keeping the show on the road: the role of the acting headteacher', *Educational Management and Administration*, Vol. 31, No. 1, pp. 67–81

Draper, J. and McMichael, P. (2003b) 'The rocky road to headship', *The Australian Journal of Education*, Vol. 47, No. 2, pp. 185–96

Draper, J., O'Brien, J. and Christie, F. (2004) 'First impressions: the new teacher induction arrangements in Scotland', *Journal of In-service Education*, Vol. 30, No. 2, pp. 201–23

Draper, J. and Sharp, S. (2006) 'Continuity and change: the initial impact of the post-McCrone Agreement', *Scottish Educational Review*, Vol. 37, pp. 99–112

Duncombe, R. and Armour, K. (2004) 'Collaborative professional learning: from theory to practice', *Journal of In-Service Education*, Vol. 30, No. 1, pp. 141–66

EPPI (2004) The impact of Newly Qualified Teacher induction programmes on the enhancement of teacher expertise, professional development, job satisfaction or retention rates: a systematic review of the research literature on induction. London: EPPI Centre, Institute of Education

Feldman, D. C. and Brett, J. M. (1983) 'Coping with new jobs: a comparative study of new hires and job changers', *Academy of Management Journal*, Vol. 26, No. 2, pp. 258–72

Fink, D. (2005) *Leadership for Mortals*, London: Paul Chapman

Forde, C., McMahon, M., McPhee, A. and Patrick, F. (2006) *Professional Development, Reflection and Enquiry*, London: Routledge

Forrester, V. and Draper, J. (2005) 'The professional formation of teachers in Hong Kong: a dim-sum model?' *Teacher Development, Vol. 9, No.* 3, pp. 413–28

Gatherer, W. (2003) 'Scottish teachers', in Bryce and Humes (eds) (2003), pp. 1022–30

General Teaching Council for Scotland (1990) *Report on the Management of Probation*, Edinburgh: GTCS

General Teaching Council for Scotland (2002) *The Standard for Full Registration*, Edinburgh: GTCS

Gewirtz, S. (2002) *The Managerial School*, London: Routledge

Goodson, I. (1994) 'Studying the teacher's life and work', *Teaching and Teacher Education*, Vol. 10, No. 1, pp. 29–37

Goodson, I. F. and Hargreaves, A. (eds) (1996) *Teachers' Professional Lives*, London: Falmer

Gronn, P. and Rawlings-Sanaei, F. (2004) 'Principal recruitment and leadership disengagement', *Australian Journal of Education*, Vol. 47, No. 2, pp. 172–84

Guest, D. E. and Conway, N. (2002) *Pressure at Work and the Psychological Contract*, London: Chartered Institute of Personnel and Development

Guest, D. E. and Conway, N. (2004) *Employee Well-Being and the Psychological Contract: A Research Report for the CIPD*, London: Chartered Institute of Personnel and Development

Hargreaves, A. (1994) *Changing Teachers, Changing Times*, London: Cassell

Heilbronn, R., Totterdell, M., Bubb, S. and Jones, C. (2002) 'The whole-school management of induction: central factor for success', paper presented at the British Educational Research Association annual conference, Exeter, September

Hersey, P. and Blanchard, K. H. (1988). *Management of Organisational Behaviour*, New Jersey: Prentice-Hall

Hirsch, E., Koppich, J. and Knapp, M. (2001) Revisiting what States are doing to Improve the Quality of Teaching, Seattle: University of Washington: Centre for the Study of Teaching and Policy

Hopson, B. (1986) 'Transition : understanding and managing personal change', in Herbert, M. (ed.) (1986) *Psychology for Social Workers*, London: Methuen, 133–57

Hoyle, E. (1969) The Role of the Teacher, London: Routledge and Kegan Paul

Huberman, M. (1993) *The Lives of Teachers*, London: Cassell

Humes, W. (1986) *The Leadership Class in Scottish Education*, Edinburgh: John Donald

Humes, W. and Bryce, T. G. K. (2003) 'The distinctiveness of Scottish education', in Bryce and Humes (eds) (2003), pp. 108–18

Ingvarson, L. (1998) 'Professional development as the pursuit of professional standards', paper presented at the Professional Standards and Status of Teaching conference, Edith Cowan University, Perth, Australia, February

Jahoda, M. (1982) *Employment and Unemployment*, Cambridge: Cambridge University Press

James, C. and Whiting, D. (1998) 'The career perspectives of deputy headteachers', *Educational Management and Administration*, Vol. 26, No. 4, pp. 353–62

Johnson, S. M. and Birkeland, S. E. (2003) 'Pursuing a "sense of success": new teachers explain their career decisions', *American Educational Research Journal*, Vol. 40, No. 3, pp. 581–617

Jones, K. and Alexiadou, N. (2001) 'Travelling policy, local spaces', paper presented at the Congres Marx International 111, Paris, September, cited in Ozga (2005), p. 208

Keddie, N. (1971) 'Classroom knowledge', in Young, M. F. D. (ed.) (1971) *Knowledge and Control: New Directions for the Sociology of Education*, London: Collier-Macmillan, pp. 133–60

Kelchtermanns, G. (1993) 'Getting the story: understanding the lives', Teaching and Teacher Education, Vol. 9, No. 5, pp. 443–56

Kelchtermanns, G. and Ballet, K. (2002) 'The micropolitics of teacher induction: a narrative biographical study on teacher socialisation', *Teaching and Teacher Education*, Vol. 18, pp. 105–20

King, M. B. and Newmann, F. M. (2001) 'Building school capacity through professional development: conceptual and empirical considerations', *International Journal of Educational Management*, Vol. 15, No. 2, pp. 86–93

Kirk, G. (1988) *Teacher Education and Professional Development*, Edinburgh: Scottish Academic Press

Kirk, G., Beveridge, W. and Smith, I. (2003) *The Chartered Teacher*, Edinburgh: Dunedin

Academic Press
Kuzmic, J. (1994) 'A beginning teacher's search for meaning: teacher socialisation, organisational literacy and empowerment', *Teaching and Teacher Education*, Vol. 10, No. 1, pp. 15–27
Lacey, C. (1977) *The Socialisation of Teachers*, London: Methuen
Lave J. and Wenger, E. (1991) *Situated Learning: Legitimate Peripheral Participation*, Cambridge: Cambridge University Press
Louis, M. R. (1980) 'Surprise and sense-making', *Administrative Science Quarterly*, Vol. 25, pp. 226–51
MacDonald, A. (2004) 'Collegiate or compliant?: primary teachers in post-McCrone Scotland', *British Educational Research Journal*, Vol. 30, No. 3, pp. 413–33
Maccoby, E. E. and Martin, J. A. (1983) 'Socialisation in the context of the family: parent–child interaction', in Hetherington, E. M. (ed.) (1983) *Handbook of Child Psychology* 4, New York: Wiley, pp. 1–102
McNally, J. (2002) 'Developments in teacher induction in Scotland and implications for the role of higher education', *Journal of Education for Teaching*, Vol. 28, No. 2, pp. 149–64
McNally, J. (2006) 'From informal learning to identity formation: a conceptual journey in early teacher development', *Scottish Educational Review*, Vol. 37, pp. 79–90
McNally, J., Boreham, N., Cope, P. and Stronach, I. (2003) 'Researching early professional learning', paper presented at the British Educational Research Association annual conference, Edinburgh, September
Maslow, A. H. (1954) *Motivation and Personality*, New York: Harper and Row
Meaning of Work International Research Team (1987) *The Meaning of Working*, New York: Harcourt Brace Jovanovich
Menter, I. (2002) 'Border crossing: teacher supply and retention in Scotland and England', *Scottish Educational Review*, Vol. 34, No. 1, pp. 40–50
Menter, I., Hutchings, M. and Ross, A. (2002) *The Crisis in Teacher Supply*, Stoke on Trent: Trentham
Menter, I., Mahony, P. and Hextall, I. (2004) 'Ne'er the twain shall meet?: modernising the teaching profession in Scotland and England', *Journal of Educational Policy*, Vol. 19, No. 2, pp. 195–214
Mercer, D. (1996) 'Can they walk on water?: professional isolation and the secondary headteacher', *School Organisation*, Vol. 16, No. 2, pp. 165–78
Ministerial Council on Education, Employment Training and Youth Affairs (Australia) (2003) *A National Framework for Professional Standards for Teaching* (online). Available at URL: www.mceetya.edu.au/mceetya/default.asp?id=11582#Teachers%20and%20teaching (accessed 20 July 2006)
Ministry of Education: New Zealand (1999) *Professional Standards: Criteria for Quality Teaching*, Wellington: Ministry of Education
National Association of Public Administration (1997) *Managing Succession and Developing Leadership: Growing the Next Generation of Public Service Leaders*, Washington, DC: NAPA
National Board of Professional Teaching Standards (2002) *The Five Propositions of Accomplished Teaching* (online). Available at URL: www.nbpts.org/about/coreprops.cfm (accessed 18 March 2006)
National Council of Teachers of Mathematics (1991) *Professional Standards for the Teaching of Mathematics*, Reston, VA: NCTM
Ng, H. M. (2001) 'A model on continuous professional development of school leaders', *International Studies in Educational Administration*, Vol. 29, No. 2, pp. 73–87
Nias, J. (1989) *Primary Teachers Talking*, London: Routledge and Kegan Paul
Nicholson, N. and West, M. (1989) Managerial Job Change: Men and Women in

Transition, Cambridge: Cambridge University Press
O'Brien, J. and Christie, F. (2005) 'Characteristics of support for beginning teachers: evidence from the new induction scheme in Scotland', *Mentoring and Tutoring*, Vol. 13, No. 2, pp. 191–205
O'Brien, J. and Torrance, D. (2005) 'Professional learning for school principals: developments in Scotland', *Education Research and Perspectives*, Vol. 32, No. 2, pp. 165–81
Organisation for Economic Co-operation and Development (2002) *Attracting, Developing and Retaining Effective Teachers: Country Questionnaire: (UK)*, London: DfES
Ozga, J. (2005) 'Modernising the education workforce: a perspective from Scotland', *Educational Review*, Vol. 57, No. 2, pp. 207–19
Paterson, L. (1997) 'Policy making in Scottish education: a case of pragmatic nationalism', in Clark, M. and Munn, P. (eds) (1997) *Education in Scotland: Policy and Practice from Pre-School to Secondary*, London: Routledge, pp. 138–55
Paterson, L., Brown, A., Curtice, J., Hinds, J., McCrone, K., Sprostrik, D. and Surridge, P. (2001) *New Scotland, New Politics*, Edinburgh: Edinburgh University Press
Pearson, M. and Robson, D. (2005) *Experience of the Teacher Induction Scheme: Operation, Support and CPD*, Edinburgh: GTCS
Poppleton, P. and Riseborough, G. (1990) 'Teaching in the mid-1980s: the centrality of work in secondary teachers' lives', *British Educational Research Journal*, Vol. 16, No. 2, pp. 105–24
Porter, L. W., Lawler, E. E. and Hackman, J. (1975) *Behaviour in Organisations*, New York: McGraw Hill
Purcell, J., Kinnie, N. and Hutchinson, S. (2003) *Understanding the People and Performance Link: Unlocking the Black Box*, research report, London: Chartered Institute of Personnel and Development
Purdon, A. (2003a) 'A national framework of CPD: continuing professional development or continuing policy dominance?', *Journal of Education Policy*, Vol. 18, No. 4, pp. 423–37
Purdon, A. (2003b) 'The professional development of teachers', in Bryce and Humes (eds) (2003), pp. 942–51
Purdon, A. (2004) 'Perceptions of the educational elite on the purpose of a national framework of continuing professional development (CPD) for teachers in Scotland', *Journal of Education for Teaching*, Vol. 30, No. 2, pp. 131–49
Quality Assurance Agency for Higher Education (2000) *Quality Assurance in Initial Teacher Education: The Standard for Initial Teacher Education in Scotland – Benchmark Information*, Gloucester, QAAHE
Raffe, D. (2000) '*Investigating the education systems of the UK', Oxford Studies in Comparative Education*, Vol. 9, No. 2, pp. 9–28
Ranson, S. (2003) 'Public accountability in the age of neo-liberal governance', *Journal of Education Policy*, Vol. 18, No. 5, pp. 459–80
Riddell, S., Tett, L., Ducklin, A., Stafford, A., Winterton, M. and Burns, C. (2006) *Gender Balance of the Teaching Workforce in Publicly Funded Schools in Scotland,* research report for Scottish Executive Education Department, Edinburgh: SEED
Rippon, J. and Martin, M. (2003) 'Supporting induction: relationships count', *Mentoring and Tutoring*, Vol. 11, No. 2, pp. 211–26
Rippon, J. H. and Martin, M. (2006) 'What makes a good induction supporter?' *Teaching and Teacher Education*, Vol. 22, pp. 84–99
Robson, D. and Pearson, M. (2004) 'The Standard for Full Registration: evaluation of current practice in the teacher induction scheme in Scotland', paper presented at the British Educational Research Association annual conference, Manchester, September
Sharp, S. and Draper, J. (2000) 'Leaving the register: Scottish teachers lost to the

profession 1997–8', Journal of In-Service Education, Vol. 26, No. 3, pp. 247–66
Schein, E. H. (1988) *Organizational Psychology*, 3rd edn, Englewood Cliffs, New Jersey: Prentice-Hall
Scottish Executive Education Department (2000) *A Teaching Profession for the 21st Century* (McCrone Report), Edinburgh: Scottish Executive
Scottish Executive Education Department (2001) *A Teaching Profession for the 21st Century: Agreement Reached Following Recommendations Made in the McCrone Report*, Edinburgh: Scottish Executive
Scottish Executive Education Department (2002) *Standard for Chartered Teacher*, Edinburgh: SEED
Scottish Executive Education Department (2003) *Continuing Professional Development for Educational Leaders*, Edinburgh: SEED
Scottish Executive Education Department (2005) *Ambitious Excellent Schools: The Standard for Headship*, Edinburgh: SEED
Scottish Office Education Department (1993) *Guidelines for Teacher Training Courses*, Edinburgh: SOED
Scottish Office Education and Industry Department (1996) *How Good is Our School? Self-Evaluation Using Performance Indicators*, Edinburgh: SOEID
Scottish Office Education and Industry Department (1998a) *Guidelines for Initial Teacher Education Courses in Scotland*, Edinburgh: SOEID
Scottish Office Education and Industry Department (1998b) *Standard for Headship*, Stirling: SQH Unit
Sennett, R. (1998) *The Corrosion of Character*, New York: W. W. Norton
Serafini, F. (2005) 'Taking on the National Board for Professional Teaching Standards: alignment, recognition and representation', *Current Issues in Education*, Vol. 8, No. 15, 20 July (online). Available from URL: (accessed 18 March 2006)
Sikes P., Measor, L. and Woods, P. (1985) *Teacher Careers : Crises and Continuities*, London: Falmer
State of Queensland (2005) *Professional Standards for Teachers: Guidelines for Professional Practice*, Brisbane, Department of Education
Teacher Training Agency (1998a) *National Standard for Special Educational Needs Co-ordinators*, London: TTA
Teacher Training Agency (1998b) *National Standards for Subject Leaders*, London: TTA
Teacher Training Agency (1999a) *Teacher Induction Guidelines*, London: TTA
Teacher Training Agency (1999b) *National Special Educational Needs Specialist Standards*, London: TTA
Teacher Training Agency (2001) *Induction Standards*, London: TTA
Teacher Training Agency (2003a) *New Induction Standards*, London: TTA (online). Available at URL: (accessed 11 July 2006)
Teacher Training Agency (2003b) *Qualifying to Teach: Professional Standards for Qualified Teacher Status and Requirements for Initial Teacher Training*, London: TTA
Tickle, L. (2000a) Teacher Induction: The Way Ahead, Buckingham: Open University Press
Tickle, L. (2000b) 'Teacher probation resurrected: England 1999–2000', *Journal of Education Policy*, Vol. 15, No. 6, pp. 701–13
Totterdell, M., Heilbronn, R., Bubb, S. and Jones, C. (2002) *Evaluation of the Effectiveness of the Statutory Arrangements for the Induction of Newly Qualified Teachers*, London: DfES (online). Available from URL: (accessed 11 July 2006)
Veenman, S. (1984) 'Perceived problems of beginning teachers', *Review of Educational Research*, Vol. 54, pp. 143–78
Victorian Institute of Teaching (2003) *Standards of Professional Practice for Fully Registered Teachers*, Melbourne: VIT

Victorian Institute of Teaching (2004) *Supporting Provisionally Registered Teachers: A Guide for Planning Induction and Mentoring Programs in Victorian Schools*, Melbourne: VIT

Walker, A., Stott, K. and Cheng, Y. C. (2003) 'Principal supply and quality demands: a tale of two Asia-Pacific states', *Australian Journal of Education*, Vol. 47, No. 2, pp. 197–208

Washington State (2005) *Effective Support for New Teachers in Washington State: Standards for Beginning Teacher Induction*, Silverdale: Center for Strengthening the Teaching Profession

Wilkin, M. (1999) *The Role of Higher Education in Initial Teacher Education*, Occasional Paper No. 12, London: Universities Council for the Education of Teachers (UCET) (online). Available at URL: (accessed 18 March 2006)

Williams, A., Prestage, S. and Bedward, J. (2001) 'Individualism to collaboration: the significance of teacher culture to the induction of newly qualified teachers', *Journal of Education for Teaching*, Vol. 27, No. 3, pp. 253–67

Williams, T. R. (2003) 'Ontario's principal scarcity: yesterday's abdicated policy responsibility – today's unrecognised challenge', *Australian Journal of Education*, Vol. 47, No. 2, pp. 159–71

Wilson, V., Hall, J., Davidson, J. and Lewin, J. (2006) *Developing Teachers: A Review of Early Professional Learning*, Glasgow: Scottish Council for Research in Education

Wiseman, S. and Start, K. B. (1965) 'A follow-up of teachers completing their training', *British Journal of Educational Psychology*, Vol. 35, No. 3, pp. 342–61

Youngs, P. (2003) *State and District Policy Related to Mentoring and New Teacher Induction in Connecticut*, report prepared for the National Commission on Teaching and America's Future, January

INDEX